Breathe In the Joy

My Soul's Earth Journey

JANICE E. CLARK

BALBOA.PRESS
A DIVISION OF HAY HOUSE

Balboa Press books may be ordered through booksellers or by contacting:

Balboa Press
A Division of Hay House
1663 Liberty Drive
Bloomington, IN 47403
www.balboapress.com
844-682-1282

Print information available on the last page.

ISBN: 979-8-7652-4035-9 (sc)
ISBN: 979-8-7652-4034-2 (hc)
ISBN: 979-8-7652-4033-5 (e)

Library of Congress Control Number: 2023905019

Balboa Press rev. date: 03/23/2023

Dedication

Breathe In the Joy is dedicated to those who are searching for signs that their loved ones in spirit are nearby. Allow the signs to surface to an open mind. May you be blessed with success.

Contents

Acknowledgements

Everyone needs and appreciates moral support. I would like to extend a thank you to those who assisted me in my efforts to complete this item on my Bucket List. It has been a challenge that has brought me great satisfaction and a new glimpse of who I am.

Thank you, Jen for your name and the cover design for *Breathe In the Joy*.

Thank you, Bob and Jen for positive feedback after reading the drafts of my manuscript. I respect you as writers as well as family.

Thank you, Carl for always believing in me. You are the best.

Thank you, Suzanne Giesemann for inspiring me to write about *My Soul's Earth Journey*.

Thank you, God for every aspect of my Being. I love You.

THE SOUND AND SITE OF IMPACT PRODUCED GOOSEBUMPS. IT HAD happened again. Another dream had manifested into reality. It was a sunny day, road conditions good, and minimal traffic on an otherwise busy road. A young male driver in a black Jeep Wrangler veered off the road and snapped the telephone pole across from my house. He was propelled out of the vehicle and lay on the lawn – exactly as foreseen in my recurring dream. *Breathe In the Joy* advocates that joy can be extracted from any situation, even this accident. The details are revealed on later pages. Have you ever experienced precognition? It is but one of the concepts addressed in this book, and quite thought provoking.

I am Janice, a soul here on the Earth experiencing a human lifetime. As I start to write about my journey, I am wondering what kind of message I will share with you, the Reader, that will bring you enlightenment, peace, validation, or even inspiration to write about your own unique Earth Journey. My hope is that you will allow your moments of joy to balance out the moments of stress; that you will see the humor in situations that irritated you when they occurred yet were inconsequential to who you are; that you will open your heart and mind to the possibility that there is connection to spirit which takes us beyond our five senses. My inspiration came from my experience in Boone, North Carolina, in 2022, when I attended a retreat presented by Suzanne Giesemann, a widely known Evidential Medium and Soul Awareness Coach. She stated that everyone has a story. That happens to be a perception quite commonly expressed. However, hearing it this time prompted me to write about my transition into connecting with spirit. Her workshop validated so many incidents that have occurred over the years that could be categorized as coincidences by some, but were synchronous events revealed by Divine Design. Of that, I am sure.

Though I am not a world-renowned celebrity to any degree, I am unique and presently living my linear age of 81 years among the Earth family that I love very much. I am grateful for this amazing last phase of my journey which began on June 3, 1941, at 5:45 A.M., in Brockton, Massachusetts.

When a soul decides to experience a Human Lifetime, it agrees to take on a human body. It starts the journey in the warmth and safety of a mother's womb only to be strenuously pushed through a narrow birth canal to an abrupt halt of the comfort and warmth of that womb. There the story begins. The bright Light of the Spirit Realm is replaced by the alternating light and darkness of the Earth plane. The journey consists of multi-faceted choices that will eventually bring the traveler back to the bright Light of the Spirit Realm, and God.

I was told by my mother that my birth process was easy on both of us. Her grandmother had come to her in a dream and handed her a baby girl wrapped in pink swaddling. Because the birth of my older brother had been a difficult breach birth, my mom was feeling apprehensive about my arrival. Her grandmother assured her that everything would be fine. Thankfully for both of us, it was.

Family Background ...

WORLD WAR II HAD NOT YET ENDED AND A THIRD CHILD, A SECOND son, would be born in 1943. Three children, wartime, unemployment, and one income to support the family. Struggling times. There was widespread unemployment and financial hardship. My father managed to always find work, including a civilian job working in the U.S. Naval shipyard in Quincy, Massachusetts. He was a machinist and maintained the accuracy of the firing mechanisms on the guns of warships.

My parents moved to a small town next to my city of birth. Our home was modest and so were those of our neighbors. Everyone was in the same boat, so to speak. I don't recall the concept of keeping up with the Joneses a big problem back then. I was a young child being a child. I had no idea of the hardships my parents were facing post-war. My parents managed. All was well.

There seems to be a basic formula for an Earth journey. The experience starts with our arrival at birth. Our world is small, and we are the center of it, a whale in a puddle. Soon we find ourselves ushered outside of our home into a much larger world. Stepping into that larger world can be both exciting and frightening. We are assured that we will love going to school where we will make new friends, and learn how to read and write. Attending church will teach us about God and the Bible. What we are not told that in the larger world we are reduced to a minnow in Lake Superior. Thankfully, we can swim.

Whale to minnow ...

WHEN IT CAME TIME FOR ME TO ENTER FIRST GRADE, I DIDN'T WANT to go. It was unthinkable. I was happy being a whale. My big brother, already a minnow, was entering third grade and seemed happy to be in Lake Superior. He begrudgingly took me by the hand and pulled me along with him to school. It wasn't cool to be attached to a little sister in public. He dumped me off at the door and I was on my own. I wanted to cry but did not dare. I tried to focus on Mom's promise that I would like school. She was right. I not only liked school, I loved school. My teacher's name was Mrs. Ryan. She liked all of us. She was very kind and smiled a lot. At dismissal, I ran the full three blocks home, burst through the front door, and announced that I was going to be a teacher someday, just like Mrs. Ryan. That announcement no doubt pleased my mother. It was her first choice for my future because it would provide financial security. She was maintaining the post-war concern for financial security in my behalf. I am happy with my memory of that first day of school because it tells me I made my own career choice. That's important to me. My mother was a strong personality and very persuasive.

My mom did a good job brainwashing me into thinking I was smart. It was fortunate that I believed her because I was very shy and was cursed with the propensity to blush when put in the spotlight. I was always worried that my face would catch on fire, or my pounding heart would burst out of my chest right in front of everyone. Or, what if I fainted? With such drama you would think I became an actor, but no, I became an elementary school teacher, hopefully much like Mrs. Ryan.

Right through high school the blushing still haunted me. In my English classes I wrote out what were supposed to be oral reports and passed them in. By doing so, if the work was in an A category, I took an automatic B grade. I was okay with that because I was not willing to stand and talk in front of the class, even though it included most of my friends. You can imagine how horrified I was my freshman year of college when, in the first semester, I had to take a course in public speaking among total strangers. I survived. Today there are many people who will attest to the fact I have mastered the art of talking. However, the spirit of testament may vary a tad from person to person.

My childhood expanded and became much more complex as the years passed by. Before I knew it, my journey exploded into adulthood where there were so many choices to make. An independent career? Marriage? Children? Retirement? Financial safety? Financial risk? Life was getting complicated.

Looking back ...

AFTER THE END OF THE WAR (1945), PEOPLE TRIED TO PICK UP THEIR lives and secure buying power through finding a permanent job, perhaps even accumulate savings. More and more women entered the workforce to increase the household income. That was a cog in the wheel of my life that I remember clearly. My mom going to work led to the divorce of my parents. It brought to the marital plate some unpalatable meals. Though difficult for all of us to digest, I mention it because it led to a gift from God that would affect my spiritual beliefs as they unfolded on my journey. The gift was my great-aunt, my maternal grandmother's sister. She moved in with us to help my mom run the household and take care of us kids. She was a registered nurse, recently retired from the school system in Everett, Massachusetts. Though she had no children of her own, she had a knack for opening a child's heart and filling it with love. Her arrival was the epitome of the expression *God is good*. What an amazing gift. My brothers and I loved her until death did us part in 1960. Both have joined her in the Light. I continue to hold her in my heart here on the Earth plane until my journey ends and we reunite.

It's a cliché, but it is said there's a flip side to every coin, and looking back, I can see that there is truth in that statement. God took incredibly loving care of us. Our family unit was interrupted by the divorce, but love was not lost. The loss of Dad in the household, which we didn't fully understand at the time, was buffered by the arrival of a 5'2" powerhouse of love housed in the body of Auntie Hekkie. I still smile at the very thought of her. She may have been short in stature, but she had a gigantic heart.

Without fail, she escorted us to church every Sunday and endured how fresh my younger brother and I were when we giggled with embarrassment because she sang the hymns so loudly during our church services. The choir director invited her to join the choir because her strong alto voice would have been an asset to a choir made up of mostly women. She gracefully declined and continued to belt out the hymns as part of the congregation while we kids continued to exchange little grins.

What I loved most about going to church was the music and hymns sung by the congregation. I felt happy, safe, and loved with each word that floated through the air to nestle in my ears. Yes, I did also listen to the words from the Holy Bible. But the music … so beautiful in sound and message. One of my all-time favorites said this:

> What a friend we have in Jesus
> All our sins and griefs to bear.
> What a privilege to carry
> Everything to God in prayer
> Oh, what peace we often forfeit
> Oh, what needless pain we bear
> All because we do not carry
> Everything to God in prayer.

My church was a small Baptist Community Church, open to all who were seeking Divine Guidance and God. It was a typical Protestant church, a white wooden building with a tall, magnificent spire which I was told, and believed, was a finger pointing to God. I have seen so many fingers pointing to God as I have traveled throughout New England and the South. I never tire of seeing them and I point them out to whomever I happen to be with.

When I was about 12, I decided, with great trepidation, to audition for the Junior Church Choir. I, who blushed incessantly and refused to speak in school, wanted to walk down the center aisle of my church wearing a choir gown, knowing that all eyes would be upon me. I knew I couldn't sing well, but I decided to go for it. It was a church. How could the choir director turn a child away? Auntie Hekkie and Mom supported that stance. We were right. The choir director did not turn me away. Instead, she quietly took me aside and very kindly told me to lip sync. My feelings weren't hurt at all, and I got very good at it. I might have been a little embarrassed back then, but today I smile at how joyful I felt to be part of the choir. Life was, and still is, good.

To be honest with you, and myself, I still cannot carry a tune unless it's sheet music. It does not stop me, though. I sing in my car, in the shower, when I rake leaves, and any other time when I am alone. If the radio hits me with a tune I know, the volume goes up and I belt out my version of the melody. I know God doesn't care if I'm off tune. In fact, I think He gave me a scale to which only the Angels can sing. My advice to you, dear Reader, is to go ahead and sing your heart out. It feels wonderful, believe me. Even in my eighties, I rock it! (Privately, of course.)

God is Love ...

As the years passed by, I developed a distinct perspective on sin that differed from that taught through the church, my mom, and Auntie Hekkie. Those three sources of guidance were stern when it came to what constituted sin and punishment. I began to second guess all my decisions. Had I committed a sin? If so, I feared facing a punishment to atone for it. It was a heavy, uncomfortable feeling to envision God as a punisher when I knew in my heart and soul that God is Love. Yet fear of being punished was being instilled in me. I began to think that every disappointment in my life was happening because I was not a good person, not because I may have simply made a poor decision for a moment in time.

I couldn't accept that an innocent six-year-old girl could sin enough to warrant a much older man from the neighborhood putting his hands on her body to molest and hurt her. It wasn't in keeping with my soul's knowing, so in my twenties, I separated myself from my church, but not from God. My love and gratitude for God's blessings have never waned. I took with me many beautiful connections to God and the Angels. I still smile and look up when I see a white spire pointing towards Heaven. I still feel the miracle of my first Communion when an unexpected flow of warmth and love washed over me as I swallowed the wine (grape juice). I was twelve. It was total peace, a feeling I am positive will usher me out of this lifetime when I am called Home.

I felt that peace a second time, in 2010, when my younger brother Al passed. I had received a call from his family that I should come to say goodbye. He only lived about five miles from me, but in my rush to get there I was driving faster than the 30-mph speed limit. I heard a voice calmly whisper, "Slow down." It was followed by that same beautiful peace I felt at my First Communion. It washed over me with so much love. I knew my brother was sharing the love he was receiving as he closed out the human experience of his Soul and stepped back into the Light.

The Golden Rule ...

MY BIBLICAL STUDY WAS NOT FOR NAUGHT. I EASILY EMBRACED THE concept of what is known as the Golden Rule. It had become a way of life and a focal point of my ever-evolving philosophy. Both Matthew 7:12, and Luke 6:31, state the ethical principle of treating others as you would like to be treated. There is a variation of wording from one source to another, but the concept is very clear. It enables me to give and receive love.

When you feel good receiving love you simply start to give love. Think about how simple actions show love, things like a wave, a hello, a phone call, or a smile. Any small gesture that produces a few seconds of joy to another person becomes monumental in the moment. And those small gestures are free to give away.

This poem called *Smiling* will bring you a smile. Read it aloud.

> Smiling is infectious; you catch it like the flu.
> When someone smiled at me today, I started smiling too.
> I passed around a corner, and someone saw my grin.
> When he smiled, I realized I had passed it on to him.

I thought about that smile, and then realized its worth.
A single smile, just like mine, could travel round the
Earth.
So, if you feel a smile begin, don't leave it undetected.
Let's start an epidemic quick and get the world
infected.

Author Unknown

There are so many occasions that pop up and give us the opportunity to treat others as we would like to be treated. Forgiving, sharing, helping, and praying for others come to mind. And do not overlook random acts of kindness.

Kindness has always been a front-runner for me. It costs nothing to be kind. It feels like comfort food, warm and delicious when you share it. Philosopher William James said: *There are three important things in life. The first is to be kind. The second is to be kind. The third is to be kind.* That is it in a nutshell for me.

My writing debut occurred when I was in the first grade and wrote a poem to my mother.

Roses are red,
Violets are blue.
You are my mother,
And I love you too.

She taped it on the refrigerator for all to see. I was famous. An author. And there it began – my desire to write. I wrote dozens of stories and poems as a child but saved only my mom's poem. Being young and innocent is such a short part of the journey called Life, and so readily transformed by the bombardment of societal expectations and pressures in the current century. I feel blessed to have had a childhood without technology replacing Nature's playgrounds. And yet, change is inevitable. The children of today can't miss something they have not experienced. So, each generation will find its own joy.

When I started teaching, I often wrote stories or poems that supported the classroom curriculum. Occasionally, I would read one to my class and let the story trigger their experiences. (It was not a new concept.) An example would be a story I wrote entitled *Happy Little Sad Cloud* which was about rain. The splashing-in-the-puddles stories led to listing how rain is helpful to the Earth. Each child had input, and their input was expanded by another child. The kids were teaching each other, pleased with how much they already knew, and soaking in some new information. They also learned the courtesy of allowing a classmate to speak his or her opinion, uninterrupted. I only had to guide them with questions and validate their reasoning. Oh, and add my two cents, of course.

There was ample resource material available to coordinate with the curriculum and as I became more deeply entrenched in my position, I neither had the time nor the luxury to do free-lance writing. There was just too much to do. I was teaching full time, running a household, and raising two children. The busy-ness of life warranted putting writing on hold but, because I am a huge advocate for journaling, I found the time to journal.

Random Acts of Kindness...

AFTER MY RETIREMENT IN 2000, I GOT INVOLVED IN PROMOTING random acts of kindness. I developed a fictional character named RAK. Those are his initials, and they stand for Random Acts of Kindness as well as his name, Roscoe Arthur Krueger. I had struggled to find a name that started with R that fit my character until I heard my mom's voice whisper, "Roscoe." My mom was in spirit at the time, as was her younger brother Roscoe. It was perfect.

I had my first children's book, *Roscoe is a RAKster,* published in 2010. It coined the terms RAK and RAKster. A RAKster is anyone who performs (random) acts of kindness without forethought. In the story, Roscoe helps his family with chores and receives unexpected rewards for doing so. It usually works that way in life for all of us. When you give to others with no strings attached, something good will manifest later for you.

My niece Jen created a puppet of RAK that took my project to a higher level. Although my ability to be a ventriloquist was somewhat limited, I gave it a shot and discovered I had a substantial level of ham in me. It was so much fun. Kids are wonderful. They loved RAK while he reigned. I wrote a modified rap song, *Do You Give a*

RAK, which my granddaughter Peyton, who was eight at the time, recorded onto a CD. Her uncle Bob strummed an accompaniment for her. It had become a family-supported project. I felt joy.

The week of February 14th is Random Acts of Kindness Week. For several years, the first-grade teachers at the Halifax Elementary School invited me to visit as a guest author during RAK Week. We worked as a team to encourage the children to write stories, poems, and songs, or perhaps use their gift of art to illustrate books. They shared what random acts of kindness they had performed at home and in school, and planned some acts of kindness they would surprise their family with over school vacation the following week. The children were delightful. They planned a surprise for me. All five first-grade classes gathered in the gymnasium where, under the direction of their music teacher, they sang my rap song, *Do You Give a RAK?* I felt joy.

A random act of kindness on my part that has been a long-term blessing occurred in April of 1989, when I met a sweet little girl from China who entered my fifth-grade classroom mid-year. She was eleven years old and spoke no English when she stepped off the plane onto American soil. How wonderful that a smile from the heart speaks louder than words. That's the way it was when I met Wing. When we smiled at each other, I felt my heart open wide with compassion, and felt hers open wide with trust. I must admit I also felt a moment or two of sheer panic because she didn't understand English, but she did understand my smile of welcome. Little did we know that a lifetime friendship had begun. At this writing she is forty-five years old. After her graduation from high school, we started celebrating her birthdays by going to lunch and a movie.

Each morning, out of respect, she bowed before entering my room and repeated her English greeting, "Good morning, Mrs. Clark." To be honest, I thought it was an adorable cultural behavior. Her cousin was also placed in fifth grade, because he spoke English very well and could interpret for her. Being bi-lingual, and a friend as well as cousin, he was a major asset to her learning the school rules and the language of her new country. However, to this day she attributes learning English to having had me for a teacher. The following year she attended a different school, but she came back to help me organize and close my classroom for the summer. An act of kindness I appreciated, first because she did a very good job, and second because she had stolen a piece of my heart. She appeared year after year to help close out my classroom, and she always wore a big smile. Matters of the heart surpass cultural differences. Coming from two very different backgrounds never affected our relationship. She was a child, and I was a teacher, honored to have her in my life. She continues to bring me joy.

I see Wing as a beautiful soul living an Earth life as a child now encapsulated in the body of a female adult. Fortunately, my child within is alive and well and totally enjoys going with her to see movies such as *Peter Rabbit, Paddington, Kung Fu,* and movies based on Dr. Seuss books. Our relationship has been both social and trusting. It has given her some moments of reprieve in her struggle to fit into an adult world. She has opened my capacity for compassion ten-fold. I can feel her frustration of having learned a lot, yet not enough for a smooth life-journey. I also firmly believe that God is holding her hand.

There are two of us on whom Wing has put a claim for being her best friends. Her other source of joy and safety is her guidance counselor from Junior High School, Miss Janet. I have no doubt that she is Wing's Earth Angel. She has been an invaluable advocate to the well-being of Wing. She has shown love and compassion consistently over the years. Her professional background has opened many helpful doors for her. She always has her back. Wing loves and trusts her beyond words. God is good. He knows just who to bring forward when there is a need for calmness and love to offset a tumultuous life. When you can't think of something to do, a simple smile can work miracles. What a gift! Give it away.

Enter Ego ...

THE GOLDEN RULE IS SO SIMPLE THAT IT IS, AT THE SAME TIME, difficult. Why? Enter Ego. Ego is a cog in the wheel of life, everyone's life. How Ego is managed determines how smoothly our Earth journey progresses. It works hard at stopping us from staying focused by supplying us with countless distractions that take us off course. The biggest setback, or delay, is often caused by stepping into someone else's story.

Egoism often gets confused with good self-esteem. Egoism is the tendency to be self-centered, fostering a "look-at-me-and-what-I-can-do" personality. Self-esteem is accepting your Self, your personal identity and character unique to you, and presenting it with love to others. Ego tries to control, dominate, and direct your Self. It wants to be in charge. It distracts by creating endless mind-chatter that produces disappointment, anger, judgment, envy, even unfounded suspicion of betrayal. All these feelings create unnecessary drama between us and members of our family and friends. When Ego gets my attention, it is always a troubling feeling. I recognize it for what it is, a waste of energy and a sidetrack on my path. Thankfully, my Soul vibration is much higher than that of Ego, and I can regain control over my Self when I am drawn into someone else's story. Yes, it has happened on many occasions, but I recognize the tactics of Ego much more readily these days. It's an ongoing struggle to stay the path.

Life is about choices. I've made quite an assortment of them in the last eighty years. It tickles my fancy to be able to say that. Imagine being blessed with this long, linear lifetime in a healthy human body. The results of some of my choices have been a bit challenging along the way, but they have led me to choose joy because I have learned that there is a positive to every negative. Look for it.

Speaking of making choices, let us look at the mythical contents of Pandora's Box, which is supposedly the origin of the seven deadly sins. Back in the 7th century BC, the Greek poet Hesiod wrote about the creation of Pandora. It was a first-woman story that parallels the Judeo-Christian story of Adam and Eve. Pandora was created by the Greek god, Zeus. He gave Pandora a very keen sense of curiosity which was put into play years later when Zeus felt wrath and anger towards Prometheus and his brother. When Pandora married the brother of Prometheus, Zeus gave her a box as a wedding gift and told her not to open it. (The box was really a jar with a lid; the Greek word jar was mistranslated) Zeus knew that Pandora's curiosity would not be denied. He had filled the box with wrath, gluttony, greed, envy, sloth, pride, and hope. As planned by Zeus, her curiosity got the best of her, and she opened the box releasing the strange gifts into the world. But hope remained contained. She had closed the box as soon as she realized what she had done.

My point in telling part of that story is my statement that there is a positive to every negative. Wrath, by a dictionary definition, is any action carried out in great anger, especially in punishment, towards another. Anger doesn't make anyone feel good, nor does expressing it dissolve it, but it often leads to forgiveness, which is a feel-good response for both parties. Forgive. Even if the other person does not know you did, his or her soul knows, and so does yours. It will bring joy. Breathe it in.

Gluttony was related to the feasting celebrations in Ancient Greece. What was served, to whom, and how much was a status symbol. The feasts provided overeating and a wasteful excess of food to impress the guests. The positive side to that? There lies the opportunity to measure healthy portions and share the excess with those who hunger, be it family or strangers.

Greed was released from the box in the mythical story, and sadly it blatantly manifests in today's world. Greed is an excessive desire to get or have assets, particularly wealth, with no thoughts of others' needs. The polar response to greed is the loving heart of those who are eager to share what they have, no matter what size the purse. *The Law of Attraction* (Esther and Jerry Hicks) tells us that what we give we shall also receive when needed. That sounds like a win-win to me. Be careful, though. If you give purposely to receive, you will not.

Envy is a feeling of discontentment and ill will that manifests when tracking another's advantages or possessions. Envy does not serve me, nor will it serve you. We are neither in control of another's accumulation of assets, spending or buying habits, or personal relationships, nor is anyone in control of ours. Divine Guidance is in play for all of us. When I look in the mirror, I only see myself, a soul who is having a human experience. I am blessed with surroundings that are mine to share with my family. I have no idea what my neighbor has, or is sharing with his or her family. It does not affect my journey unless I allow Ego to convince me otherwise. Ego wants "poor me" to kick in. So, what is the positive? Step back and take a closer look at your blessings. Appreciate what is yours and express gratitude. *Breathe In the Joy.*

Sloth, by a dictionary definition, refers to one who is disinclined to work or exert oneself. It represents laziness. A better interpretation for the twenty-first century is sloth's suggestion to slow down and enjoy your life's journey. What is the rush? Divine design will get you where you are going. Trust.

The last deadly sin revealed was pride. Pride in its harsh definition is exaggerated self-esteem that often results in arrogance. It's all about one-up-man-ship. We encourage our young people to take pride in themselves and their achievements, and rightly so, but we also teach them to be grateful for the opportunities that come their way. No haughtiness. Good self-esteem comes from respecting your Self and your actions. Let excessive pride stay with the lions.

Hope was the seventh deadly sin, but it was not released by Pandora. Did Zeus intend there would be no hope for the world, or was hope yet to be opened to save the world? We would have to time-travel back to the 7th century to find out, but because I believe in positive outcomes, I will embrace the latter.

There is much Greek, Roman, and Norse mythology that spills into the flow of civilization to offer explanations as to why civilization has evolved to be as it is. The month of January is named for the Roman god Janus, protector of gates and doorways, and transition. He is mostly known to the average non-historian for being depicted with two faces, one looking into the past, the other looking into the future. The two faces of Janus are the symbol of the astrological sign

Gemini, my astrological sign. Some say one face lies and the other counteracts with the truth. But, what if one face does look back and reviews the past, and the other looks forward and sees another dimension? The two faces of Janus represent abstract dualities which date back to a time before Romulus and the Roman Empire. Perhaps lies vs. truths was one of them as told in the interpretation for the sign of Gemini. Another example is life vs. death. A modern version of an abstract duality is that of our five earthly senses vs. expanded senses that allow us to connect with spirit. This Janice believes that multi-sensory expansion is being revealed world-wide in Divine Time, that a shift in consciousness is underway, and that the sins let loose from Pandora's box will be returned, enabling Hope to be set free.

Life is about choices

I SAID EARLIER ON I AM JANICE, A SOUL EXPERIENCING A HUMAN lifetime. My 81 years have been comprised of choices made by me, executed by me, experienced by me. Those choices were followed by more choices made by me, executed by me, and experienced by me. Whether consciously or unconsciously, I have been processing *should-have* and *shouldn't-have* choices probably all my life. The choices I have made, or not made, have brought me to who I am. I like myself. The choices were mine to make and I accepted responsibility for the outcomes. There was no need for anyone else's approval. Choices made from the heart source are never wrong. Each was correct, and all yielded a lesson learned. My journey is unique to me. Your journey is unique to you. There may be similarities, but there is no cloning.

Although I try to stick to the plot of my personal story, I have on occasion allowed myself to be drawn into someone else's drama. My Ego convinced me I could help direct their course to the correct outcome. It caused me sleepless nights and constant mind chatter trying to create a scenario that would bring about the solution I thought was right. I was taking on the responsibility of making choices for someone else's Earth experience, choices that weren't mine to make. The day came when I asked myself, "Who am I to judge what is right or wrong for someone other than myself?"

Matthew 7:1 *"Do not judge, or you too will be judged."* gave me a little nudge. I had taken a detour from my own Earth journey. Fortunately, I learned to step back and be a listener, rather than a solver. When a person needs to air a problem, he or she may not be looking for an opinion. Expressing concerns aloud gives the speaker an opportunity to hear the problem, too. I find that when I mull a problem or situation over and over in my mind, it gets worse. When I speak the problem, I also hear it. It loses some of its punch and brings the situation into alignment with a solution.

I am aware that this lifetime is not a bowl of flawless cherries. The lighter shades of red are not ripe, while others are deep red and luscious looking. All cherries contain pits which could chip a tooth or house a worm. Still, I gladly put my hand into the bowl and choose the one that seems to call my name. I anticipate the taste of the sweet juicy flesh that will soon bring me satisfaction. If its juices drip onto my favorite shirt, so be it. Another laundry item. Everything comes out in the wash. Did that last comment trigger a memory of your mom or grandmother? She is saying hello.

While there is little joy in the pits, a positive attitude can soften the blow we create for ourselves when we choose the wrong cherry. Or is there even a wrong cherry to choose? Every choice is a learning experience. There is nothing wrong with that.

The title of my book, *Breathe In the Joy*, simply means to *Ac-cent-tchu-ate the Positive* as suggested in the 1944 song written by Harold Arlen (music) and Johnny Mercer (lyrics). It has been recorded by many celebrities of the music genre. Bing Crosby comes to mind for me. If you know it, go ahead, sing it. When I find the positive in a negative situation, and there is one, it brings a moment of joy. Recognizing and embracing moments of joy generates gratitude, trust, and appreciation for life as a human. It gives a reason to smile. If you *Breathe In the Joy*, you will manage to get through anything.

I always turn to God for help when there is serious drama that affects me or those I love. I totally trust placing myself, or them, in God's hands. Someone tucked this prayer into a gift I received. The author is unknown.

> *Dear God, no matter what difficulties I face, I know You are always watching over me, leading and guiding me in ways that give me hope. Thank you for never letting go of my hand.*

I have shared that prayer several times. It is not important for the recipient to remember who sent it. The message is what is important. We are of God. Of course, He is holding our hand. His touch is called Trust.

Author your own story ...

TAKE A STEP BACK. ARE YOU AUTHORING YOUR OWN STORY, OR ARE you too busy trying to reconstruct the plot of someone else's story? Ego will point out flaws in others and urge you to straighten out their journeys. It nudges us to think we can change another person's path, for the better of course, because we have so much control of our own path. Know that we cannot make changes for anyone except ourselves. Proceed cautiously. If you are criticizing someone's life choices and pointing out a new direction for him or her, Ego has your attention. Every human being is orchestrating his or her own human experience. Put your energy into developing the plot and events in your own Book of Life. Allow others to do the same for their book. Because we are all of God, Divine Guidance will guide us on our journey back Home, and into the Light.

Faith and trust are paramount as I continue to move forward on my journey. There have been some crooked paths, some hills to climb, some holes to climb out of, some disappointments, and some sadness, all offset by moments of joy. Divine Guidance always gently pushed me in the direction that was right for me, that brought me comfort in hard times, and most importantly, gave me the capacity to forgive and be grateful. When I complete my journey, I will be a Soul whose Earth experience expanded my Spiritual Being and I will be happy to go back into the Light.

Discovering spirit ...

HINDSIGHT IS A WONDERFUL THING. I HAVE LEARNED SO MUCH ABOUT myself during flashbacks to events gone by. Some events I managed well; others were plain disasters. Always, at some level, I knew a greater Source was guiding the outcomes. I am sure Ego has prompted others to have track my successes and failures and openly critique them along the way. It is a human thing. What they didn't do was feel and absorb the results of my choices, choices that made me stronger and made my lifetime more purposeful. They were unaware that I owe no explanation for any action they perceived as wrong. They were unaware that my Spirit Guides and Isaac were with me every step of the way. Loving me. Directing me.

My spiritual path began dimensional changes about 40 years ago when I joined a community of women associated with a local New Age shop. The women I met there were wonderfully positive in actions and attitude. I had found a much-needed space in which I could open my wings and soar with Spirit. I realized there is more to life than what I was perceiving through my five senses. A feeling of serenity took over when I realized there is so much *knowing* in my soul. Spirit is real. I *know it*. The knowing came when Isaac made himself known to me. Isaac is my guardian angel.

My mom and Auntie Hekkie had always told me that we have guardian angels who watch over us. I wanted to know mine on a more intimate level, so during a meditation I specifically asked for its name. I wanted to give us a more Earthy relationship. I clearly heard Isaac. Angels are androgynous, neither male nor female, however, I feel a strong male energy when we talk. I have given Isaac the pronouns he and him and his. Calling him by name allows me to have an intimate grasp on our relationship. I know he is with me every moment of every day. I know he is a grantor of protection, love, and guidance. All I need do is ask and Isaac will respond. Angels abound and will always respond. It is their pleasure. Make a connection and *Breathe In the Joy.*

Intuition ...

ONE OF THE SPIRITUAL GIFTS GIVEN US FOR OUR EARTH JOURNEY IS intuition. According to **Webster's New World Dictionary** intuition is *the direct knowing or learning of something without the conscious use of reasoning.* It's that gut feeling when you sense something is good or bad. You can't quite explain how you knew an event would occur, but you knew, and it did. It's a wonderful tool to use when making choices. The negative is Ego. It will rear its head and try to talk you out of trusting your intuition. How many times have you made a choice that you knew was wrong, but did it anyway? You thought you were reasoning it out, but you weren't. It was Ego interfering. Intuition is always correct. We must learn to trust it. It is a life lesson.

I have chastised myself on many occasions over the years for not trusting my intuition. Fortunately, after I kick myself soundly in the derriere, I can forgive myself and change direction. Changing direction is not always easy, so listen up and trust that mysterious little nudge that urges yes or no in your mind. I'm in my eighties and still working on it. Just a suggestion. Your choice.

Not heeding intuitive flashes can cause round-abouts in life. For example, I knew my former husband was way out of my league when he invited me out on a date. He was four years older, was being discharged from the Army, and had far more life and relationship experiences than I had experienced, including a previous engagement to be married. Major vs. Minor League was very apparent on our first date. We went into Boston to a cabaret, which turned out to be very provocative for a country mouse. I was a product of an overprotective helicopter mom and aunt, the proverbial small town country bumpkin out in the big city lights. It was my first experience with exotic dancers and breasts being shaken at the audience, and I was with a man I didn't really know. I must credit him with being very quick to see my discomfort. He kept the conversation flowing with his eyes on only me. I knew I was treading on thin ice, and I surprised myself when I accepted the second date because I harbored a general distrust towards all men at that time of my life.

I had only graduated from high school the previous year and had started my sophomore year in college. We married in my junior year. Two sons, a teaching career in motion, and twenty-five years later we separated. It was inevitable. I had gotten lost in the vastness of his personality. What is important is that I learned to recognize my Self. In doing so, it enabled him to choose between a second bachelorhood and the confines of a marriage. Life is about choices. And so, it was.

My lifetime still includes efforts to recognize and trust my gut-feeling. Sometimes it's a chill, sometimes a voice, or a vision that catches my attention, but I have learned to stop, look, and listen before crossing the tracks.

The formula ...

GETTING BACK TO THE GENERAL FORMULA I DISCOVERED FOR MAKING my way on the Earth Plane, mine looks like this in an outline form.

Birth

Childhood

Schooling

Workforce/career

Marriage/two children

Divorce

Spiritual Awakening

Remarriage

Retirement

Death pending

The outline is quite common. You and I might have similar experiences, but as more details are added, the uniqueness becomes apparent. Everyone has his or her own story and it is ever changing. You are the author of yours. When your story doesn't serve you, change the plot. When a character becomes an energy vampire, bid that person adieu. It is a fixable cog in your wheel. Keep rolling.

Nothing about entering the Earth plane is simple. The formula contains an innumerable number of details. For example, my paternal grandfather was the oldest of thirteen children. My father was one of five children. I was one of three children. My Grandpa's story is far different from mine, yet it has had a huge influence on the unfolding of my life's journey. He was a wonderful family-oriented person, warm and kind. I missed out on a close relationship with him because of my parents' divorce. (I was ten.) He was incredibly special to me even though I had such a brief time frame in which to know him. Though he smoked cigarettes, I remember him for his pipe. He was handsome, and that pipe tickled my fancy. He looked like a movie star. I even liked the smell of the burning tobacco. It was not the offensive smell of cigarettes. It was fragrant. I liked the way the smoke curled, and the big puffs of smoke he blew out towards the ceiling made me laugh. I thought his eyes twinkled when he smiled. That was certainly intriguing. However, it was his kindness and gentleness that drew me to him.

Grandpa was born in Middleboro, Massachusetts. His parents owned and worked on their family farm. I remember going there when I was young. There was an outhouse in the backyard, several yards away from the house. It was a two-seater. There was a half-moon cut out of the door to let light in and let the awful smell out. To use it at night, a lantern or flashlight was necessary. And what about the cold of winter? A horrifying thought. I was about seven years old and was appalled to think two people would sit over a hole in a bench and poop together. Later when I needed to use the bathroom, I panicked. My mom saved me with the good news that the family had installed a modern flushable toilet inside the house like the one in my house. That was when I began to appreciate the comforts in my life.

My connection to Grandpa was not entirely lost. My present home is a non-smoking zone, yet I often smell cigarette smoke when I am watching TV. I feel certain it is my grandfather dropping in to say hello. It is not unusual to smell a scent that is connected to someone in spirit. With my mom, it is her perfume. There is comfort in the validation that our loved ones are nearby. My soul knows. It brings me joy.

Family values ...

THE YEAR 2022, IS ENDING. I DARE SAY MOST FAMILIES WITH CHILDREN have both parents in the workforce outside the home while someone is paid to care for the children in their absence. This can be problematic because the family values are at risk of not being taught and family traditions often get lost. I was very disappointed that my father was missing, but we were blessed with Auntie Hekkie, our powerhouse of love. She was all about family values. She expressed gratitude for each day, apprised us of the presence of angels protecting us, taught us good manners and kindness toward each other, and reminded us that God loves all His children, no matter what the circumstances. She also reminded us that God always knew what we were up to. We could not hide.

There's that guilt again, imposed automatically, just in case we went astray. I must admit it did keep me thinking about my actions and reactions. It was the early connection to my church that gave me the foundation for my moral compass, which is still in good working condition, well supported by my dedication to the Golden Rule. Walking away from my church did not affect my level of love and respect for God and the way I choose to live. And having a bar of soap thrust into my mouth because I told my brother to go to hell wasn't God punishing me. It was my mom. I can laugh at it now, but it was gross at the time. I choose joy to balance out the difficult spots that show up on my journey. And I never forget that God is holding my hand.

Expressing gratitude was also instilled in me as a child. I am so grateful that I was able to embrace the value of gratitude at a young age. It is embedded in my Soul and has spilled nicely into the makings of my human mind and body. Over the years, I have written personal journals filled with gratitude for my many blessings. I have also encouraged family and friends to keep a journal. You have probably read these words, as I did on a Face Book entry, though perhaps paraphrased: "When you end each day with an assessment of your blessings, the next day starts on a positive note." I have no idea who is being quoted in some fashion, but the concept is universal and widely shared on social media, and at retreats and seminars. It resonates with me. This Earth journey is so complex that I find joy as a simple way to stay on track. Gratitude is fundamental to a smooth journey.

Synchronicity ...

SOME PEOPLE SAY SYNCHRONICITY IS A SERIES OF COINCIDENCES. Coincidences are random events that occur in a series. They happen by chance. Synchronous events occur in a series also, but there is a design to them. I have found that even when events unfold in mysterious ways, they always have a positive to balance out a negative. That is not a coincidence. That is Divine Design.

In 2001, I traveled with three of my friends to the Navajo Indian Reservation which covers desert territory in Arizona, New Mexico, and Utah. The trip included a horseback caravan onto the desert followed by a sleep-over under the stars. That's where I met Benny Boy, my transportation into the desert. I had asked for a slow, older horse that might be ready to retire because I was inexperienced and feared that I would not be able to control a more spirited horse. My childhood fantasy of being Annie Oakley flashed through my mind as I hoisted myself aboard Benny Boy. It looked a long way down to the ground. I wanted to use Annie's stick-horse to gallop onto the desert, but feeling Benny Boy moving beneath me brought me back to reality. The horse was acting fidgety as we were setting up the caravan. I took in a long deep breath and exhaled slowly to calm down. There was no point in me being anxious, too. I had made the decision to join the caravan, and I was ready to go. Best of all, I knew Isaac was with me.

At the outset, the Native American guide asked everyone carrying a purse to leave it in a locker. Everyone except me. I had on a fanny pack. He told me to turn it to my backside away from Benny Boy's head in case something in it would make noise due to the bouncing of a trot. Noises distract the horses.

Seventeen riders, plus two guides, started the ride onto the desert. My uneasiness about being on a horse subsided substantially when the first awesome sight was a monolith of reddish-brown stone which centuries ago had thrust itself up from the desert floor. It reached high into the sky, boldly standing in the flat vastness of the desert, glistening in the sunlight. It was magnificent. There were two crows, or ravens, nesting at the top. One kept flying down at the caravan, cawing loudly. My intuition kicked in and I knew someone was in trouble. It was the same feeling that had given me a chill nine months earlier when we decided to make a visit to the Navajo Reservation for an overnight under the stars. At the time of planning, it just didn't feel right to me. What if one of us got hurt? The girls assured me nothing would happen. With muffled hesitance, I agreed to the plan.

I was last in line by choice because I did not want to hold up the line. One of the two guides also rode at the back end of the line. I asked him if he knew what Crow was saying. No answer. I told him someone was going to take a fall. He grunted and rode off towards the middle of the line.

Then it happened. My fanny pack had twisted back to my front. A container of Tic-Tac mints rattled in the fanny pack and the lead rope fell loose from the pommel. It dangled between Benny Boy's legs. Spooked, he reared onto his hind legs throwing me off as he lunged forward. I had started to fall off on the left side onto the low vegetation, but someone pulled me back upright and dropped me onto the soft, sandy berm on the right side of Benny Boy. When my friend Linda rode up to check on me, she started to go into low sugar shock. The Tic-Tac container that caused my fall held the sugar that kept her from passing out. Had I not fallen, no one would have known sugar was available. A series of coincidences? Perhaps. But I can still feel the pressure on my arm that pulled me to a safer landing. I am sure Isaac was protecting me. And though both my body and pride were injured, there was a positive to every negative. Divine Design. Synchronicity.

Another example of synchronicity were the events of my dear friend Julia's passing. She was ninety-eight and a half years old at the time and was as sharp as a tack. She was an amazing, complex, generous, strong, woman who was somewhat a workaholic, but filled with fun that spilled out whenever we were together. We laughed a lot and even burst into song on occasion. Our favorite was *Que Sera Sera*. She was one of the few people who heard my unique singing voice. No lip syncing. I figured that anyone who made the best grilled cheese and tomato sandwiches ever, and burgers smothered in onions that were to die for could handle an off-key song. I remember a somber moment when she asked me if I would forget her when she was gone. "Not in this lifetime, my Friend, not in this lifetime," I replied. She had a piece of my heart.

I was not going to see her that day in August when she fell and snapped her femur. I was going to attend a cook-out at my sister-in-law's house, but Julia had called to see if I could give her a hand in the morning taking yard waste to the local dumping site. When we returned to her house, we decided we could also get in a cup of tea before I had to leave. There was a step-down going into her breezeway. She fell off the step and was taken by ambulance to the hospital where she underwent two surgeries. One was a pacemaker, on Monday, followed by surgery on her leg on Tuesday. She came through both very well. I was relieved when I had Wednesday to hang out with her. I smiled at the thought of celebrating her ninety-ninth birthday come January.

The nurse called me early Thursday morning. Julia wanted me to come to her room right away. It was 7:30 A.M. when I got there. She told me that she was going to pass that day and wanted to say thank you and goodbye. I calmly said, "You're welcome, but let's see what the day brings." We both knew she had come to the end of her Earth journey.

I stayed and dozed off in the chair by her bed. Something stirred me awake and I saw her sister and mother, both in spirit, standing by the bedside. There was a man at the head of her bed leaning over the raised-up mattress being playful. I had met her sister before she passed and had seen pictures of her mother, but I did not know the man. He turned out to be her husband. She never talked about him beyond the sadness of telling me he had passed three months before I met her. They were married fifty-six years. I was careful not to ask personal questions and intrude on her privacy. Her niece showed me a picture of him when we were sorting out her belongings before the sale of her home. He was the man I saw being playful. He had come with her sister and mom to help her pass. There was no surprise when I got the call a few minutes after midnight telling me she had passed. Her soul's Earth Experience had come to an end, just when she knew it would, and she had gone safely back to the Light.

Synchronicity by Divine Design: an unexpected morning call followed by an unexpected fall at home; an ambulance ride to the local hospital, two surgeries, and her announcement three days later that the time had come to leave the Earth plane. All these events were followed by the gift of seeing her family nearby to usher her into the Light. It was a miraculous gift. I had promised she would leave with love and be greeted with love by those who left before her. We both shared that belief. What validation. Life is full of surprises. I felt joy embroiled in the sadness of my loss.

Finding and creating joy …

LOOK AROUND YOU AND MAKE A LIST OF THE SIMPLE THINGS THAT bring you joy, things that bring a smile or trigger a fond memory. Right now, on this sunny, crisp October day, I am looking at a festive Fall wreath with a transparent plastic pumpkin in its center. The pumpkin lights up. The glow is just as sparkly in daytime light as in evening light. Orange and red leaves and bright yellow sunflowers make up the wreath. I am blessed because this wreath represents the kindness and love of my sister-in-law Hazel, who gifted it to me in celebration of Fall.

On the table beside me there is a plush, stuffed animal, a representation of a sloth, a little three-toed creature native to Central and South America that moves slowly and deliberately in the trees. It represents my brother, who is in spirit. The months before his passing were frustrating for him because he was weak and couldn't move quickly, even with a walker. He would get discouraged and call himself a sloth. It wasn't too much longer before he traveled the last steps of his journey back to the Light, and God. He was called Home on Flag Day, June 14. It was an appropriate day on which to end his human experience because he had felt privileged to serve our country in the U. S. Army. With his Honorable Discharge in hand, he had continued to live an honorable lifetime among his family and friends, loved by all.

Even though I know he is safe and well, I asked for a sign that he is around me in spirit. He sent me a vision of a sloth. A sloth? Well, I started to see them everywhere. They were featured in ads on TV, pictures on cards and gift bags, covers on journals, pictures on calendars, and as subjects of animal documentaries. Whenever there is a sloth-sighting of any kind, I say hello and smile. It brings me joy.

My family in spirit is always nearby. That is a given for me. However, I also have partnered with Mother Nature and planted a tree or flowers in their memory. My younger brother Al is represented by my Forsythia bushes, the shoots of which were taken from the bushes at his house after he had passed. My first yellow flower of early spring is Al saying hello to me. It's so much fun to discover that first yellow blossom. I *Breathe In the joy.*

For my older brother (I am a sloth), my sister-in-law helped me remove about a dozen Day Lily bulbs from their garden. I planted them along my backyard fence. I take a picture of the first blossom each year, a bright orange flower, followed by many more. They bring me joy.

Before my dad passed, he gave me a sprig from a shrub growing in front of his house. He claimed I could put it directly into the soil, and it would grow. Well, I did, and it did. After his passing it grew like wildfire. I look at it each day when I go out my front door and smile. I do not know the name of the shrub. It is unimportant to me. Its deep green foliage is beautiful and healthy, just like he is in Spirit. That belief brings me joy.

There is a large lilac bush on the side of my driveway. The flowers are lavender in color. It spreads with new shoots and needs to be thinned out regularly. I replanted one of the shoots in a new spot in memory of my mom. She loved the strong scent of lilacs in Spring. She used to make a bouquet out of them and place it on her table. I thought the scent was overwhelming in a closed room, but she loved them. Her choice. Her journey. Her joy. While I do share her love for the fragrance of the lilacs, I prefer it wafting in the breeze outside of the house. My choice. My journey. My joy.

I have a Rose of Sharon tree planted on the side of my house. It is in memory of my former husband, the father of my children. He had planted a row of Rose of Sharon at his house after we had separated. It was my favorite tree back in those days. Though it would be presumptuous to say that he did it for me, he did know I would be delighted. I was, and now he has another one from me. It is all good. It brings me joy.

I'm still searching for a perennial to plant in memory of my friend Julia. I know she loved roses, but my thumb is not green enough to take them on. Mother Nature brings perennials into bloom on schedule. It would be easier for me if I could find the perfect plant. However, even my intuition has not kicked in with a name for the mysterious perfect plant, so every year, in her memory, I plant Impatiens, another of Julia's favorite flowers. They thrive nicely alongside my Begonias. I suspect that she is very happy with me getting my hands dirty in the soil when I plant. She always felt good when she gardened. The dirtier she got, the happier she was. Her memory brings me joy. The fact that the Impatiens thrive brings me even more joy.

For Auntie Hekkie I offer up an assortment of church hymns (no lip syncing) in my car, or when at home alone. Sometimes I hum them when I am out and not too near anyone. I really cannot resist my favorites. I think she sends them to me because singing brings me joy, which is a big component of my balancing life strategy.

Hang on to the memories that bring joy. Be aware of their source. Joy is not about money, although an unexpected windfall would certainly trigger a joyous feeling. Joy is happiness felt in simple pleasures that originate from love. Joy is a feeling that accompanies giving or receiving. It is warm and satisfying. Allow it to surface, even in the face of sadness. Sometimes being silly, or sentimental is just what the doctor ordered. Go plant a tree and give it a name. Just a suggestion. Your choice.

Can't sing ...

THIS WHOLE "CAN'T SING" SITUATION HAS BEEN A NUISANCE MOST OF my life. A few years back, I realized that there have been a series of events that attempted to seal my coffin of song. I think it began back when my cousins and I sang for Santa Claus. He visited us at my paternal grandparents' house on Christmas eve. He had an exciting "Ho! Ho! Ho," and his eyes seemed to twinkle. I was always a little off key on the Christmas carols, so my mom told me to just move my lips. Next was the choir director at church who had welcomed me, but also instructed me to lip sync. Oh my, and I had almost forgotten about Mrs. G., the music supervisor to our teacher in elementary school. I found her to be a terrifying woman. She would walk up and down the aisles and lean over to hear us sing. If someone did not sing the high notes correctly, she would pull their hair until they were standing up and had reached the high note. It always happened to at least one of my classmates on her once-a-month visit. I was devastated for them. She was my biggest nightmare. I do not know how I managed not to be heard. Luckily, for a couple of her visits I was absent from school, happy to be ill.

Years later, I was drawn towards getting certified to practice hypnotherapy. I had met Carl and felt like I had known him before.

Frivolously, I thought perhaps my interest in hypnotherapy would yield a past life connection to Carl. It did not. A shocking component was the surface of the man who molested me as a child. The memory cannot be erased. On that occasion, however, I felt strangely safe. I knew Spirit had handled the situation for both of us. It was time for me to forgive this man for a violation that negatively impacted my life. In forgiving him, I was released from the anger associated with his transgression. My initial intent to learn about hypnotherapy was a lighthearted, personal curiosity about past-life experiences. I did not expect to explore experiences of my present life. My interest in hypnotherapy brought me a gift of healing. Divine Design.

As students, we hypnotized each other. In one of my sessions, I was taken back to a time when singing was an issue. That session released the memory of Mrs. G. embarrassing me in front of the entire class. My face was bright red, ready to burst into flames, and my heart pounded in my chest. Tears rolled down my flaming cheeks and certainly must have given off steam. It all came back to me. My biggest nightmare had taken place. I had blocked it out. I had no idea that I was one of her victims until that moment. Unfortunately, the knowledge did not also release a melodic voice hidden in my vocal cords, but it did have an important positive. As a teacher, I tried very hard never to force any of my students to speak (or sing) in front of a group until they felt ready. After all, Mrs. Ryan would never have done that. And that resolve was strengthened by the final nail that tried, but failed, to secure my coffin of song.

It was in 1963, that I began my teaching career in Brockton, Massachusetts. I was so excited, and a little anxious, too. My first choice was third grade and that was the position open to me. At that time, elementary school teachers taught all the extra-curricular subjects: gym, art, health, and music. Yes, my contract required that I teach music. And that responsibility brought me in contact with a music supervisor who would come once a month to check on my class's musical skills, just as Mrs. G. had done back when I was in fifth grade in another town. Enter Miss M., the person who was apparently destined to become my second nightmare of song. I found her to be another terrifying woman. Even the children were anxious when she came by, but to be fair, perhaps their anxiety reflected my terror. Music should be fun and bring joy. Two good things were in play. One was the children would only have me for nine months; and the second was Miss M. was going to retire soon.

Well, there she was at the back of my room waving both arms shouting, "Stop!" The class had not reached the only high note my pitch pipe could not produce. I did not think it was disastrous. It was only one note out of many songs taught. She demanded to know who taught the song. I looked her right in the eyes and calmly said, "I have been out sick, and a substitute taught the song." A bold-faced lie! Right in front of my third-grade class! The blood rushed to my face, and I lit up like a neon sign. My heart was pounding. What was I thinking? I was desperate. The childhood chant *Liar, liar, pants on fire* flooded my mind, but I held my ground. I stood tall and threw my shoulders back to feel more confident. It was too late. Karma lost no time to address the bold-faced lie. Miss M. determined I was guilty of musical ineptness on the grounds that I did not correct the error made by the sub. Punishment pending.

Miss M. took it upon herself to keep me after school to show me how to use a pitch pipe. It was a round harmonica kind of instrument that was one octave. It included flats and sharps. I used one quite efficiently because I didn't sing well. To be honest, I wasn't prepared for what came next. She blew a note on the pitch pipe and asked me what note it was. I am serious. No *Liar, liar, pants on fire* here. I knew how to read music, but name a note solely on sound? I had to admit I had no idea. After all, if I could do that I probably would have graduated from Berkley School of Music and would be teaching something more intricate than *Mary had a little lamb*. She blew another note. Nothing. How could she possibly have been so appalled? But she was. After detaining me for three sessions in one week, she gave up on me. My love for the fun of song returned and I believe it rubbed off on my students, regardless of my inability to name the notes by sound. Life was good again. I felt joy.

My search ...

IT WAS IN THE 70S AND 80S THAT I BECAME MORE AWARE OF SPIRIT. I started to investigate diverse ways that spirit makes itself known to us. I was both curious and open-minded about connecting to spirit, connections that would integrate with, and expand, what is given us through our five senses – see, smell, touch, hear, and taste. In other words, I entertained the thought of being an extra-sensory individual instead of a five sensory individual, because I am. And so are you.

I traveled many avenues in my search to connect to spirit. Each avenue led to another. The investigation became more and more interesting and complex. Possibly, one of the first places curious people check out spirit is through a card reading experience. Tarot Cards caught my attention in my early twenties. My mother got me interested. Her favorite gift was a card reading. When I booked an appointment for her, I also made one for me. It was interesting, but no one I knew, besides Mom, would even discuss such an evil, far-out thing at the time. I felt much like a rebel, but even though I was willing to unlock my early belief system taught by the church, I was in no way turning my back on God. I was exploring another dimension. I was taking baby steps onto my spiritual path. It was a long time before I realized the cards were but a tool to allow my intuition to speak louder. Sure, I took the route of memorizing the meanings of the cards as given by the creator of the deck, but after a while I was able to expand a reading with information that was not attributed to the card in front of me. Yet that card triggered my response. It was a tool that stopped the mind chatter and allowed me to focus on what was happening in the moment. I became even more intrigued by the medium. It led to my study of the Runes.

A rune is a tile, or stone, on which one of 24 characters are etched. The 24-character runic alphabet (futhark) was used by the Scandinavians and other early Germanic peoples from about 300 A.D. The runes are divided into three aetts (eights). When ordered in sequence they reveal the journey of life much like the journey of life depicted by the twenty-two cards of the Major Arcana in Tarot. They are used as a method of connecting to one's higher self, for inner guidance, or for tapping into intuition as a method of foretelling what the future may hold.

I was particularly drawn toward learning more about the runes, so I enrolled in an in-depth study of the runes at the Denali Institute of Northern Traditions in Chugiak, Alaska. The runes are based on Norse mythology with the god Odin being responsible for the origin and interpretation of the runes. The energy of the runes seemed stronger than working with Tarot. They were fascinating. However, Tarot garnered more interest than the runes, which are not well-known in our area. I stopped doing Tarot and Rune readings because there was so much more to explore on my journey. I realized I was being temporarily side-tracked.

Then, of course, there is mediumship. A medium, according to *Webster's New World Dictionary*, is a person through whom communications are sent to the living from the spirits of the dead. The loss of a loved one is no doubt the strongest incentive to learn more about spirit. Many reach out to a medium and walk away happy to know their loved one is safe and well in spirit. That decision also often leads to the seeker expanding awareness and pursuing more knowledge. It opens a path to exploring new possibilities or satisfying one's curiosity. Can we really connect to spirit? For me it was curiosity. I was already experiencing connections to spirit which I did not quite understand or know how to handle.

After the passing of my former husband, I met with Medium Tom Frederick. As I entered the room, he commented that a big guy had come in with me and was being very pushy about giving me a message. He then asked me if the name Bob meant anything to me. I explained it was my husband, a man who pooh-poohed the concept of himself making it to Heaven. The message? "Tell my wife I made it. She was right." I felt joy for two reasons. One that, of course, he was with God, and two, that was the first time he had ever admitted I was right. Because of Bob, I learned the value of moral support. He was not good at implementing it, but I am blessed with the ability to offer it when needed. The person who should have understood me the most did not understand me at all. I harbored resentment until I clearly realized we were not at the same level of spiritual development. There he was in spirit showing me he now understands my belief system. Unfiltered criticism is detrimental to a healthy self-image. Experiencing that has provided fuel for my stance on kindness.

I have been present on several occasions when a medium gathered an audience with the intention of bringing spirit through to deliver a message specific to a receiver. My initial purpose for attending was to figure out how they connected with spirit, but I kept getting a reading each time I went. Those readings validated that there was another dimension accessible to us for guidance. Most of my old-time friends pooh-pooh that idea, but we love each other anyway. I do not force my beliefs on anyone. We all progress on our path at our own rate. Luckily, I also have a group of like-minded people who understand this phase of my Earth journey because they are walking beside me on their own similar path.

One of my memorable readings occurred when I took a friend to a session hoping she would get a reading. Maureen is a well-known medium in my area and beyond. She was taking a few minutes to try to explain how she received information, which piqued my interest. She seemed a little irritated when she asked if anyone had an Al in spirit. Three of us raised a hand. She said her attention kept being drawn to the car outside the window. It was a Nissan Altima. She laughingly said an Al needed to come through and he wasn't going to be denied. We all laughed along with her. That explanation led to a pause and her comment to the Al, "Really? Who the hell would know someone named Trixie?" The other two hands went down and there I was, hand in the air and red-faced with all eyes upon me. Shades of my youth! While blushing diminishes greatly with age, it never stops entirely. It can catch you off-guard in unexpected situations. Trixie was unexpected, for sure.

Shortly before he passed, my brother Al (forsythia bush) told me he had seen and talked to our great-aunt Trixie. I doubted it initially because he was about 13 years old when she passed, and we saw little of her. She was a buyer for Bonwit Teller and lived in a brownstone on the Charles, in Boston. He described her perfectly, and even remembered where she lived and worked. It was surely Al saying hello. Leave it to him to mention Aunt Trixie to get my attention. He could always make me laugh. Maureen approached me and asked why I was there when I could connect to spirit myself. I did not have a simple response. It feels more like spirit reaches out to connect with me, rather than me reaching out to connect with spirit. Interesting.

Precognition ...

MY DREAMS BECAME MORE DETAILED AND FORETELLING. THAT IS, many became reality. It is called precognition, the perception of an event before it occurs. It can happen in a dream, intuitively, or while awake in a mind-movie. I have experienced all three.

A mind-movie is a flash of an event before it happens. For example, I was driving on Route 495 heading home from Cape Cod in Massachusetts when in my mind I saw a red car flip onto its roof and roll down an embankment on the righthand side of the road. It startled me because there was no red car in sight. I also felt that rush of fear that hits your abdomen when something unusual or frightening occurs. As I approached the top of the next incline, I saw brake lights. There was the red car flipped onto its roof. People were rushing to make sure the occupants were not hurt and call for help. There was no other car involved unless the red car swerved into a roll-over to avoid a collision with another car. If so, the other car did not stop.

My precognition dreams began to make sense. They had a negative twist that alarmed me, but I soon realized that the perceived negative twist was balanced out by a positive outcome. Perhaps the "oh no" piece was to get my attention. It worked. I also came to the conclusion that my dreams were intuition's camera.

In one of my early dreams, I saw a black Bronco, traveling too fast down East Street in my old neighborhood. It crashed into a white building. I awoke at impact in a sweat. It was so real. There was no way to tell if the driver had survived. I knew I was an observer, not a passenger. I also knew it would happen. I just did not know when or to whom.

On June 3, 1995, my older son was driving his black Bronco too fast on East Street, the exact location from my dream. He lost control. The vehicle went off the road. It became embedded into the side of a white house. His account of the incident is that he was upset at the time and driving too fast. He became aware that there was someone in the vehicle with him talking calmly about impending dangers, and a need to slow down. When the vehicle went off the road, time shifted into slow motion, and he felt a peaceful bubble form around him. There was no sound and no fear. The person in the passenger seat, who was a male energy, calmly put his hand on the side of my son's head and gently pushed him below the height of the windshield. When the crash occurred, the roof was crushed down over the steering wheel and rested on the back of the seat leaving no escape. Yet, my six-foot four son was found lying on the ground, not seriously injured, and not sure how he got there. He thought his passenger had helped him out, but when he asked the police to check on him, there was no sign of a passenger. He was alone. The peaceful bubble had dissipated. The noise and hubbub that comes with an accident, filled the air. More police and neighbors arrived, and an ambulance screeched onto the scene. In the retelling of the accident, he insists a calm voice of reason spoke in his vehicle before impact. He has no recollection beyond that. His guardian angel at work? We are loved and protected by Divine Design. The positive from the negative? My dream had manifested with a happy ending. His physical body was spared serious injury, and we both received validation that we are connected to spirit.

In another dream a Jeep Wrangler crashed into the telephone pole across from my house. It was so real that I felt butterflies in my stomach and bolted upright in my bed to avoid the impact. The next night I dreamed the same dream only there were more details to the dream. It was a black Jeep Wrangler, driven by a young man, perhaps in his twenties. The vehicle crashed into the telephone pole across from my house, but this time I seemed to be an observer rather than an occupant of the Jeep. The dream was still unnerving. It did not reoccur the next night.

Two weeks later, a black Jeep Wrangler, driven by a young man, crashed into the telephone pole across from my house. The Jeep was deemed unable to be repaired, but the driver was thrown clear and not seriously injured. What a relief. I was focused on the negative aspect of a crash and didn't take into consideration the positive side of the event, the safety of the driver and a lesson well learned. It turned out he was newly licensed and was speeding. It was a life lesson for him and prompted me to pay closer attention to my dreams.

In the Spring of 1996, I dreamed I was driving a car south on Route I- 495 toward Cape Cod. I was in the passing lane in the vicinity of the Wareham water tower. Something unexpected happened in that lane. Something came in front of me. I jammed on the brakes, felt the fear, but did not see what it was. I woke up shaking.

The next night the dream gave me more information. This time I was a passenger in the car, not the driver. It was the same stretch of road. I am in the passing lane and something totally unexpected happens in that lane. I woke up in a sweat. The dream revealed the color of the car. It was white and there were two passengers. It was particularly concerning to me because members of my family frequented that stretch of road. I certainly would not wish a disaster on anyone else, but I must admit I asked their angels to hover closely. When the details started to accumulate, I believed something was about to happen. I had no idea what it would be. It did not feel good.

The third dream had me as an observer. I was no longer inside the car. It's a divided highway in that area. Spans of open grass areas alternate with treed areas planted to cut down on the glare of oncoming traffic. Something came out of the trees. The impact woke me up. I did not see the crash.

On March 31, 1996, a small plane trying to make an emergency landing crashed into a white station wagon on Interstate 495, in West Wareham in the vicinity of the Wareham water tower. A mother and her small child were killed. The two passengers in the plane were killed also. The small airplane had lost engine power and when trying to make an emergency landing, had skimmed over the treetops that lined the median, and landed on the road directly in front of the car killing all parties. When I saw the report and pictures on the news, I knew my dream was over. I am not to know why that accident took place. I later learned that there was a third person in the car that survived. I must accept that as my positive.

It was 1996 when I traveled to Australia with my friend Judy and my niece Ellen. I must admit that I always experience some level of anxiety when I fly. I go back to my thought that if I were meant to fly, perhaps I would have wings. However, I also trust that my path has Divine Guidance, so what is there to fear?

I was not surprised when I dreamed of a plane crash the week before departure. I awoke trembling with sorrow for the families that would be impacted by the terrible news. It was so real. The plane exploded into a ball of fire. There would be no time for panic. It seemed like a missile hit the plane and caused the explosion. My husband chided me about my anxiety to fly, so I tried to set the dream aside. In the dream I seemed to be an observer and felt no impact myself. Maybe he was right; it was fear of flying kicking in. The dream took me a step beyond my intuition that something air related was about to happen, but when I thought of the dozens of possibilities, I decided to let it go.

On July 17, 1996, our flight departed Boston taking us to California. It was to be followed by our connecting flight to Sydney, Australia. On the same day, Trans World Airlines flight 800 departed John F. Kennedy International Airport to Rome with a stop in Paris. Flight 800 exploded mid-air and crashed into the Atlantic Ocean. The investigation as to cause determined that a short circuit caused a fuel tank to explode. There were many conspiracy theories, a couple of which had said a missile had struck the plane. In my dream it was a missile, but that does not make it so. I looked for a positive in the situation. I know there is one for those who were affected by the tragedy. It will surface when the pain subsides. For me, the positive is the realization that dreams can be an extension of intuition using a stronger voice. Not always, though. It's tricky to differentiate between a mind-chatter dream and precognitive dream. The precognitive dream will be laced with strong intuitive feelings. That is what is developing in me on my Earth journey.

Psychometry ...

ANOTHER FORM OF CONNECTING WITH SPIRIT IS PSYCHOMETRY. FROM Webster's New World Dictionary, psychometry is *the supposed faculty of divining knowledge about an object, or about a person connected with it, through contact with the object.* Often it is a piece of jewelry. At a girls' night sleepover one weekend, the hostess asked me to wear her father's ring to see if there was a message from him in spirit. I wore it to bed but awoke in the middle of the night and removed it because it was giving me a painful headache. As soon as I took off the ring, the pain stopped. When I related the experience to her at breakfast, I apologized for not having a message because I had taken the ring off. She said her dad had passed from a brain tumor and asked me where the pain was in my head. It was the same area. She felt sure he had made himself known. It was a new experience for me and a validation for her.

On two other occasions I experienced similar impressions with a ring. One was at a hospital when I transported my mom to the emergency room. She handed me her ring because she was thought it would be removed and lost if she were admitted as a patient. It was a rock. She had remarried a businessman who had given her a large diamond. I slipped it onto my finger for fun. Immediately I was overwhelmed with a feeling of haughtiness. I quickly positioned my hands to make sure anyone coming into the room could see the diamond. I felt snobbish and superior, which are foreign feelings to me. The feelings dissolved as soon as I returned the ring. My mom had revealed through the energy of the ring that status was important to her. I didn't realize she felt that way, but even with my dad's child support, raising three children with no financial security must have been difficult. It was an interesting revelation to surface. Even more important, the experience pointed out the shame I felt for exploiting the wealth aspect of having that ring on my finger. Yet, at the time I felt I could not control my reaction.

The second ring experience was a gift from my very dear friend Julia. She was quite financially secure. Her diamond is a rock also. I know she loved wearing it. She bought the ring just because she could. It tickled her fancy, and that makes me smile. I am a little embarrassed when I wear it because it's so big, but there are no feelings of haughtiness, only feelings of love. It makes me feel closer to her. Only calmness and approval are felt when the ring is on my finger. Two rings, two women I love very much, two entirely different stories. Interesting that both have walked beside me for a distance on my path. Life is amazing. Revelations like this bring me joy.

Signs abound ...

BACK IN 1992, I WAS TICKLED PINK TO BE INVITED TO ATTEND MY niece Jennifer's graduation from Quinnipiac College in New Haven, Connecticut. Attendance is quite limited at graduations because of space restrictions and so many eager family members who want to share in the event, so I felt very fortunate to be included. While Jen's parents and I sat waiting for Jen's group to be called forward, my sister-in-law asked me if I thought my mom, Jen's grandmother in spirit, knew Jen was graduating from college. Without hesitation I blurted out, "Absolutely!" At that very moment my necklace broke and fell into pieces in my lap. It was a necklace my mom had given me. I had intentionally worn it because I wanted her to be there. And she was!

My college friend Pat (Framingham State College) passed away in the year 2001, after several years of being treated for cancer. Her initials were PMA, which she said stood for Positive Mental Attitude. I met Pat and her roommate Judy in college. We considered ourselves a version of "the three musketeers." We banded together in our freshman year and never lost touch. We supported each other through joys and sorrows, and whatever else life threw onto our path.

Judy and I had an opportunity to travel to Australia and New Zealand with a group of educators from a nearby school system. Pat's health was failing at that time. With her blessings, we accepted the invitation. The very week we were leaving to go abroad, Pat's health took a downward dive. We were at the Taronga Zoo in Sydney on the day of her passing. Judy pointed out the giraffes and we stopped to acknowledge them by shouting out a hello to Pat. She loved giraffes. They were in framed pictures, stamped on her nightshirt, in bronze statues, and about anywhere you could add a giraffe in a home décor without being tacky. Giraffes represent standing above the crowd and seeing the whole picture. She always stood above the crowd.

Judy turned and asked, "Do you think Pat is okay?" The answer came in the form of a beautiful butterfly that came out of nowhere and fluttered in our faces and around our bodies. In that moment, we both knew that Pat's soul had ended its Earth experience and had returned to the Light. She was above the crowd seeing the whole picture.

When I remarried in 1989, my husband and I went on a cruise to Alaska. It took us North as far as Glacier Bay. The scenery was magnificent. It felt like we could reach out and touch the mountainside. Unexpectedly, a wash of sadness came over me. My longtime friend Carol and I had made a pact that we, the pathetic (not really), ditched (yes) divorcees, would take a cruise to Alaska to celebrate our fiftieth birthdays and our fabulous lives. There I was, ahead of our schedule, floating on a calm sea in Glacier Bay surrounded by breathtaking views provided by Mother Nature, seeing it for both of us. She had been on dialysis for a while and the prospect of keeping our plan had waned. Although she knew I had remarried, I hadn't had the heart to tell her our honeymoon was an Alaskan Cruise.

My thoughts were shattered when out of nowhere came a hummingbird, Carol's favorite bird. She had taken me to Newport Beach on one of my visits to California specifically to see the hummingbirds that lived in the bushes near the marina. There were hundreds of them. It was my first time getting to see them up close and personal. They were mesmerizing.

The hummingbird hovered in front of me and then disappeared. Although she had not passed, I was sure that Carol knew I was in Alaska. The hummingbird was her way of saying, "Hello, have fun." It turned out her sister's friend forwarded the news that I had remarried and was on a cruise. Carol had assumed I was in Alaska and was very excited for me. Her high energy sent me a high energy gift, the hummingbird, which represents joy. Amazing.

When my parents divorced, my brothers and I spent the token Sunday afternoons with my dad. We were fortunate to spend many of the Sundays with our paternal grandparents, my father's sister Helen, and our cousins before our teenage years crept in. When that happened, we no longer wanted to go out on Sundays with our father. Our connection to family was broken. We wanted to be with our friends. Thinking back, that transition must have been hurtful to my father, or possibly it was a relief. Later in life, he told me he was never a family-oriented person. He kind of disappeared. We only saw him on occasions to which he couldn't refuse an invitation, our graduations and weddings come to mind. He skipped over birthdays, but came by on Christmas. I kept in touch because I really liked my father. He was a good man. He had an interesting sense of humor and could always get me laughing with his zingers. He had integrity and was honest. It wasn't until his years between the ages of 80 and 93 that I took the time to really get to know him. I visited him every week and discovered an emotionally reclusive person who was not about to give up his feelings and beliefs easily.

We used to talk about an afterlife occasionally. He was raised Roman Catholic but didn't believe there is more than our physical existence. He used to say, "We live, we die, and pfft, it's over." He could not be swayed. I smile at what a nice surprise he got when he crossed over.

A few months after he passed, while driving home from the market, I asked him for a sign to let me know he was around. He sent me a mind-movie of Tom. Tom was a wild turkey that was hanging out in his neighborhood. It perched on the roof of his car, on the railing of his deck, and patrolled the small neighborhood, yard by yard, eating what we call pesky insects. When a Tom is hanging out alone, it means that he was pushed out by the competition during mating season. Eventually, the Tom is accepted back to the females and their broods. Although it is more common for turkeys to move from place to place within their territory, Tom had been lingering his roost in Dad's neighborhood.

My father thought Tom was cool. The neighbors, however, did not. Someone called the police and Tom was killed and carted away. Dad was so disappointed that a better outcome was not chosen to rid the neighborhood of a pest. That whole scenario played out in a mind-movie. I was left with a wild turkey for my sign. I burst out laughing. It was November. Of course, I would see a turkey!

Well, a wild turkey I did see. In fact, I saw flocks of them, and frequently. I never realized how many wild turkeys there are in my area. Traffic comes to a stop when they meander across a road. They do not hurry along. I am sure that it has happened to me before, but it did not register as a turkey sighting. I simply hoped they would not get run over.

I shared the story with my younger brother who pooh-poohed it immediately. He did not believe in signs. One day when he was driving home from an errand, he took a different crossover street to his neighborhood. By his own estimation, he saw at least seventy-five turkeys on someone's property. They were perched on the roof, the porch, the parked cars, and a detached garage. More were feeding on the lawn, and others were blocking the street. He was on Budd Avenue. Our dad's name was Bud. Dad had come through to him. I felt joy.

Receiving Peripherally ...

SOMETIMES, A CONNECTION TO SPIRIT MANIFESTS PERIPHERALLY. THIS happens often for me. However, I am not privy to the outcome. When I am out with, or in conversation with someone, I sometimes pick up thoughts or concerns that another person nearby is mulling over. One such occurrence took place in my dentist's office. My hygienist Kelly had lost her mom and we were talking about her passing. The name Annie (not the real name) kept repeating itself in my mind. I thought it might be her mom's name, but it wasn't. She said a coworker had a daughter named Annie. I felt sickness or special needs associated with the name. When I asked about the child, I learned she was a young teen-ager who was mentally and emotionally distressed and going through a very low time. It was the first time I had conflicted feelings. I heard "home." It was not clear if Annie's mom should go home, or if Annie was going Home. I was not sure if I should share that feeling. It's a huge responsibility to disseminate information received spiritually.

The connections can occur anywhere. Another time I was part of a meditation group I regularly attended on Monday nights. The over-all group varied in attendance from week to week. At the end of the allotted meditation time, we could choose to share whatever we had experienced with the group. I had clearly seen a map of the United States. The state of Ohio stood out. Ohio does not mean anything to me. I shared what I had seen because there was good energy around it. A young woman in the group said she was getting ready to go to Ohio to meet her fiancé's parents. She was having some anxiety about the outcome. My intuition assured her the travel would be safe and fun.

I still have a problem with peripheral connections. I do not know quite where to go with them. They can be fun, though. The day I went into the bank and asked the very pregnant teller what she was going to name her son was fun. She said she had told no one that it was a boy when she found out. The doubters would say I had a 50/50 chance of being correct, which is of course true, but I knew it was a boy. I also told her he would be healthy and well blessed. The mom-to-be was delighted. Those are happy moments. They bring me joy.

Another time, when out for lunch, I asked the waiter when he was going to start culinary arts school. It turned out he had just put in his application to Johnson and Whales Culinary Arts School in Rhode Island. There had been a delay in his attendance because of illness, but he was ready to go back. It still surprises me when I blurt out such unexpected revelations. It is also food for thought for the receiver, no matter how long it takes to digest it. A little more gravy would help.

Seeing Spirit ...

SIGNS AND DREAMS BEGAN TO MULTIPLY UNTIL ONE DAY IN MY MIND'S eye, I saw Spirit. I went into immediate denial. I was sure I was going over the edge. Strangely, I did not feel fear, just disbelief. My curiosity expanded exponentially. One occurrence after another happened and they still happen. I have been struggling with how to manage such experiences. Let's face it, saying you see dead people is not a topic of conversation you would lead with. My fear of being called crazy far outweighed my courage to talk about it.

What has saved my Earthly sanity is my discovery that many of you experience feeling spirit around you, too. Attending the retreat in Boone, N.C. placed me into a large group of men and women with whom I have a lot in common. I also believe there were a few skeptics among us. My ability to work with spirit has been validated; my comfort zone is getting more comfortable; and my personal awakening to spirit gets more fascinating every day. I have learned that it's all right to express that spirit is present when I feel or see it. My fear of ridicule is still present, but I trust my feelings and Isaac to guide me when to make spirit part of the conversation. I cannot make it happen. An appearance happens on its own and always takes me by surprise. I can see and describe what the person is wearing.

My task has become to ask questions such as, "What's the message? For whom?"

Back in 2002, when my friend Judy's daughter was getting married. It was a joyous, though hectic time. Judy was feeling a little down because she had no family left to celebrate with her. Sometimes the happiest occasions trigger Plum Land. It is what I call the four of cups in Tarot. An interpretation is "**poor little unloved me**," and yet love is always present. She was a triplet whose two sisters had passed as toddlers. Her husband had passed from cancer, both parents and a brother had passed, and she felt she was losing a daughter even though she was very happy about the impending marriage. I was driving on the highway to visit her and give some moral support when I saw, in the sky ahead of me, her family in spirit. It was like looking at a portrait. Her dad was standing with her now healthy brother, and her two now healthy baby sisters were sitting on her mom's lap. Their message was, "Tell her we will be there." I was astounded by the vision and where I was receiving it. What if I had driven off the road? How would I ever explain why I was distracted? So, I asked that spirit come to me at a safer time. That request has been honored.

Nancy ...

NANCY WAS ONLY SEVEN, A SECOND GRADER AT MY SCHOOL. SHE WAS a sweet, shy little girl with a princess look about her. Her daily complaints of a stomachache led to the diagnosis of leukemia, a devastating blow to her family. She was home schooled during her chemo treatments. It became apparent that a bone marrow transplant might be a solution to extend her life. Her brother was in my third-grade class at the time and was a match. It was such a difficult journey for the family, and for this young boy who loved and wanted to save his sister's life. The transplant did not work as hoped, and Nancy passed.

Some years later, when her brother was perhaps in his early twenties, we met again in a connect-to-spirit group led by a prominent Medium in the Quincy, Massachusetts area. We were sitting beside one another in a meditation circle, no doubt by Divine Design, when Nancy presented herself to me. She was wearing a pretty, pink party dress. Her complexion was vibrant as she skipped around the circle chanting, "Tell him I'm okay. Tell him I'm okay. Tell him thank you." When it was time to share, I disclosed what I had seen and heard. I also said I recognized the child, and the message was meant specifically for her brother who was the young man sitting beside me. I could feel him release his sense of failure as he hugged me. It was a beautiful moment for both of us.

Ken and the clipboard ...

A GENTLEMAN (TRULY A GENTLEMAN) NAMED KEN WAS THE PREVIOUS owner of my present home. He had designed and built it from the ground up. He and his wife kept the house and grounds immaculate. I used to ride by it on my way to work and always admired the property. A whimsical thought, "I would love to have that house someday," crossed my mind. It was not an envy thought. I already owned a lovely home on the south side of the city, but this one was closer to my school and would save me time, and money. And it seemed to call my name as I drove by each day on my way to work.

After my husband and I separated, a new concern needed attention. My stepfather passed. He and my mom lived in Rhode Island. I wanted to bring my mother closer, so I decided to look for a house with an in-law apartment. She would have maximum privacy, and there would be privacy for my sons and me, as well. Mama Mia! I could not believe it when I found out my dream house was for sale and it had an in-law apartment. Can you see how spirit works? Synchronicity. Divine Design at play.

Ken had purchased the lot across the street and had built a smaller home for himself and his wife. His primary home was for sale upon completion of the new house and, therefore not advertised publicly. It became available during my search. My gratitude was abundant. I was able to sell my house and purchase my new home. My mother sold her house a year later and moved back to Massachusetts into the in-law apartment.

When Ken became ill and started his battle with cancer, his daughter and son-in-law invited him and his wife to live with them. It was sad to have them leave. Ken was interesting to talk with. He always offered good advice when we chatted. He suggested, quite strongly, that every evening I walk the perimeter of my property with a clipboard to jot down the little things that needed to be done. It would avoid a larger, more costly problem later. He was correct, of course. Still, I waited a little too long on a few things. Money was not exactly flowing after my marriage ended. It was more of a drip, drip, drip.

One afternoon, just before dusk, I saw Ken (in spirit) on the sidewalk across from my home, clipboard in hand. He was dressed in his dark brown work clothes, looking much like a UPS driver. He had on his wide-brimmed straw hat which he wore when working in the sun. Though surprised to see him, I smiled and took it to mean I had better do an assessment of my property. There were a few fix-its to be done, but no major problems. I appreciated the reminder, and I remain vigilant.

One of my earliest spirit sightings occurred in my home in the 90s. There were five of us women who met once a week to explore and share activities that would help us develop the ability to connect to spirit. Even though we all are born with that ability, there are a lot of factors that can either enhance or deter our success to connect.

Mindsets produced by our general belief system, religion, fear, attitude, peer pressure, or family disapproval affect the progression of our journey towards enlightenment.

We called ourselves Sisters in Spirit, spirit referring to being like-minded. I was astonished when I saw a man of short stature standing beside one of the women. He was wearing a blue suit and white shirt open at the collar with no necktie. He appeared just when she mentioned looking into possibly becoming a pharmaceutical representative. My description fit her father who was a doctor, and in spirit. We were unsure of a message: "Yes, go for it," or "No, it's not for you right now." But it was also a validation that those in spirit are nearby and loving us.

The experience confirmed that there is more to Being than our linear lifetime. I decided to explore more deeply into the gift of higher vibration and my connection to spirit. I had said so many times that all of us can connect to spirit, yet I had questioned my own experiences for years before I accepted that we are all multi-dimensional beings. My journey is, and has been, focused on my personal development. I have studied tarot, the runes, hypnotherapy, mediumship, and I am a Reiki Master. I am still working on mastering meditation. Though I did go through a period when I offered readings for others, I seldom do readings now. However, when spirit makes itself known while with someone, I feel confident enough to speak up. Spirit reaches out only when its message is in the highest and best interest of the receiver. I trust that implicitly.

Energy and vibration are the elements that bring spirit to the foreground. Spirit has high vibration, and those of us humans that vibrate in alignment with the five senses do not. To connect with spirit, one must increase one's vibration, and spirit must decrease its vibration. When vibration is more closely aligned, there is a connection.

Opening to spirit class ...

I KNOW IT'S HEALING FOR A PERSON IN MOURNING TO KNOW HIS OR her loved one is well, but are they prepared to be told a loved one is standing beside them? To help myself deal with seeing spirit I attended an *Opening to Spirit* class held in the home of a well-known medium, Sandy. There were only eight of us, six women and two men. The purpose of the class was to recognize and expand our ability to connect to spirit. Each of us knew it can be done but struggled to believe that we were really connecting. Is there evidence?

Alicia (not her real name) was part of the class. Her plans to marry her fiancé came to a sorrowful halt when a tragic accident took her fiancé's life. She was there to connect with him. She was the first in the group to volunteer to connect, guided by Sandy. It is important to be in a group, or in a one-on-one situation where there is no pressure to share, just a desire. I looked over at Alicia who was sitting quietly with her eyes closed and saw a young adult male standing beside her with his arm around her shoulders. He was wearing khaki chinos and a green jersey. They had the same color hair and were close in complexion, as well. I thought they could be siblings. I was not trying to connect, but I saw him beside her. I did not receive a message. Learning how to receive a message from spirit was the reason I had joined the group. When I told her what I had seen, she opened her phone and showed me a picture of her fiancé dressed in khakis and a green jersey. I realized then that telling her what I had seen was the message. She had, in fact, brought him through. It was an amazing validation for both of us.

Another woman in the class wanted to know if her son in spirit had attended her daughter's wedding. I saw the inside of a Catholic church and a bride and groom kneeling at the altar. A little boy about 5 years old was running a circle around the altar and kept crawling under the drape and peeking up at the couple. He was laughing and having so much fun. After her meditation, the woman was disappointed that she had not made a connection. Feeling foolish about what I had seen, I chose not to share my vision and remained silent until, that is, she made the comment that her son had been only seven when he passed and that was probably why a connection didn't happen. My account of what I saw was a gift to her and all of us. Her tears of joy were a gift to me. Sharing that amazing experience strengthened my belief system and my courage to speak up.

On a separate occasion, I made an appointment with Sandy to meet with my special, long distance friend Marie. Marie was eager to find peace after the loss of her husband from a tragic car accident. She and I were able to talk about the accident comfortably, but when I realized Marie was open to experience a spirit counseling session, I thought Sandy was the perfect person for her to see. She is compassionate and kind. She has a sensitive, yet joyful, approach to dealing with loss because she knows there is no loss. Our loved ones are still with us.

While Marie was waiting to see Sandy, I noticed a man in spirit standing behind the woman sitting across from me. He had his hands resting on her shoulders. The woman appeared anxious as she spoke with the person who was accompanying her to the appointment. The man was stroking her back and smiling. He had on a plaid, cotton shirt with long sleeves. The colors were green, blue, and gold with a thin black line defining the squares and rectangles in the design. He wore dark pants. I could not say anything to the woman because it would not have been appropriate, given she was there to see Sandy. It made me wonder why he appeared to me at all. Working with spirit is an experiential learning process. Fascinating.

I have no problem with referring my friends to others for spiritual counseling. The sources of comfort and compassion are wide-spread and made available through Divine Design. I also set up a meeting for Marie with Roland Comtois, a medium well-known for his purple papers. The purple papers consist of hand-drawn pictures and comments that he receives psychically. He writes and draws the information on purple construction paper. Sometimes it is many months before he meets the person for whom it is meant. Marie was still seeking validation that her husband was safe and well in spirit. His paper was dated long before he met her. The accident happened in New Jersey. Roland lived in Rhode Island at that time. When he met her and connected to her energy, he said he thought he had a purple paper for her. He did. It showed the accident, the helicopter med-flight that took them to the hospital, and the family gathered around her husband's bed when he passed. She received her husband's message that he is all right and began to see signs that he was with her, starting with the robins, his favorite sign of Spring. Robins built a nest above her door. Robins and Spring are signs of new beginnings. But best of all, there is an eagle's nest in the trees behind her property. When the eagle soars, so does she. She is now privy to a bird's eye view of life, a wider spectrum of our humanity. A glimpse at being reunited for eternity.

Anthony and family ...

ONE OF MY VERY FAVORITE SPIRIT CONNECTIONS WAS MADE WHEN I was having coffee with a young man named Anthony who is expanding his spiritual awareness and working as a Life Coach. I have known him since his birth and am delighted that we can support each other on our journey. We meet regularly at a coffee shop and exchange thoughts on a variety of subjects, most related to spiritual development.

At one of our meetups, I saw an older man standing beside him wearing a Perry Como style sweater, either dark navy or black. Anthony immediately thought it was his maternal grandfather. He laughingly commented about the Perry Como sweater being his grandfather's uniform. He said it was interesting that I mentioned Perry Como because his grandfather also sang Como songs and sounded just like him. His grandfather had recorded a love song for his wife. As a hello to his grandfather, Anthony played it in his car regularly. He played it for me. It was amazing. He sounded just like Perry Como who passed in 2001, at the age of eighty-nine.

Spirit works in mysterious ways. Members of Anthony's family continue to channel through me. When his Uncle Richie (his mom's brother) passed from colon cancer Anthony was about to turn fifty, the age recommended for men to get a colonoscopy. Richie showed up to one of our meetings. I knew it was Richie, but I didn't hear a message. Anthony knew right away that Richie was there to remind him to get a checkup, which he did right after his birthday. Richie saved his life. Anthony had cancer, underwent surgery and chemo, and is now cancer free. A blessing from his uncle and friend, and God.

Anthony's Uncle Elio (his dad's brother) also made himself known to me. I was doing dishes at my home and saw him standing on the sidewalk across from my house. He had on what looked like dark green wool trousers with suspenders, a plaid shirt and work boots and he was looking my way. Elio's brother Willy (Anthony's dad) was inside my house meeting with my husband about an income tax issue. "Oh no! Now what?" was my reaction.

Elio had a message for his brother. To convince myself that this was real, I asked Elio to tell me something I did not know about him or Willy. I heard one word, scrabble. I went to the office and asked Willy if scrabble meant anything to him. He was excited to tell me his brother Elio went to his house every Sunday morning after church to play Scrabble with him. When Elio passed Willy started to visit Elio's grave every Sunday morning. Elio's message was that it was unnecessary because he was always around him.

On another occasion Elio followed Anthony into the donut shop for one of our meetups. I told him he was there but lost the connection until Anthony started telling me about a family reunion his family had recently attended in New York and how badly his dad Willy felt because his brother Elio wasn't there. Elio appeared again and said, "Tell him I was there and saw everyone."

Ashley ...

ASHLEY IS A BEAUTIFUL SOUL WHO IS IN SPIRIT. SHE WAS A LOVING, creative young woman who returned to the Light much sooner than those who loved her here on the Earth Plane had expected. The impact of her tragic drowning cast a huge shadow of "life is unfair" over family and friends. Emotions ranged from shock to anger, and from denial to despair.

The funeral service took place in a beautiful, old church in Fall River, Massachusetts. Its architecture included an amazing dome that blossomed towards the heavens. It was there, in the dome, that I saw Ashley. Her chin was resting in her palms as she lay on her stomach mid-air smiling radiantly down on us. Her mom had chosen a special music piece that Ashley loved while on the Earth plane. When the music started playing, Ashley began dancing above us like an angel on gossamer wing. She floated above us, gently moving to the rhythm of the piece, lost happily in the sound. I was amazed that no one else was looking up. The white light that enveloped her far out shown the filtered rays of sunlight shining through the stain glass windows. It was such a joyful scene and incredible experience. Tears and joy, polar opposites.

Our Chrissy ...

THE PASSING OF A LOVED ONE HAS A WAY OF CATAPULTING YOU INTO a new book, plot, and cast of characters. You have no choice. The length of the grieving process is unique to the mourner. There is no hurry, but forward is the only direction in which to go, one day at a time. Whether you write your book on paper or securely file it in your mind, the memories of love and laughter are yours to keep. *Breathe In the joy.* Store it in your heart.

In addition to being motivated to write this book after attending the retreat in North Carolina, I was also prompted to write it after the passing of my beautiful daughter-in-law Christine. In my heart I know she is healed and dancing with the angels, and that enables me to process my loss on my level of *knowing* she is healed and loved beyond our Earthly capacity to love. The effect of her passing on my son and his two children has been difficult. My grandchildren are young adults, both in college. I know they will survive, along with their dad, and come to terms with her mortality. Memory is a double-edged sword. One side is sadness. The other side is laughter. When they are ready, they will talk it out in tears, and laughter will return. Once a little laughter burps up, there will be more. It brings an understanding that all is as it should be, whether we fully understand it or not. I pray they will reach that place sooner, rather than later with the help of their angels, and the knowledge that Chrissy is still around them in spirit. It is a knowing that will slowly bring joy back in their lives.

The week that Chrissy passed, a white, downy feather floated from the sky and danced across my windshield while I was stopped at a traffic light. That little downy feather represents an angel if you believe in signs, which I do. The next day a gray, downy feather floated in front of my windshield. (Different location) It is interpreted to mean "hectic time, peace coming." Seeing the feathers prompted me to write the following message from Chrissy:

> Soft and downy, floating by
> Fell two feathers from the sky.
> One was gray – turmoil and tears,
> The other white – An angel here
> To bring back peace and soothe the pain,
> To shower love, and not the rain.
> Dancing, chanting in the sky
> "My love for you will never die."

A friend sent me a beautiful Peace plant in March after Chrissy had passed. It displayed six lovely white blossoms, but after they faded the plant didn't bloom again. My inept green thumb was no help, so I did a Sherlock Holmes and investigated why not. It turns out that the plant doesn't like the chlorine that is added to our tap water. I switched to spring water and the plant perked up. Go ahead and try it. (You're welcome.)

You already know I name my plants, so I appealed to Chrissy to push out a couple of flowers to let us know she would be with us on Christmas. On December 27, I noticed two white flowers on the plant hidden behind the leaves. Because I was distracted on Christmas day, I didn't look for them, but they were there. I am so delighted to share another sign that spirit wants us to know all is well. It gives me joy.

A star in the constellation Libra was purchased and dedicated to Chrissy by Barbara and Bob, her brother-in-law and sister-in-law. They asked me for some input as to what to write on the plaque which would then be presented to my son David and his children. This is what we wrote:

> There you are so high above,
> A shining star sending love
> To all of us as we look high
> And watch you sparkle in the sky.
>
> We return it day and night,
> Direct to you in Libra's light.
> Your spirit reigns in all of space.
> We'll ne'er forget your smiling face.
>
> Sometimes we feel life isn't fair,
> But ETERNITY is ours to share.
> So, sparkle on, shine and glow,
> Our beautiful Star to love and know.

I talk to her often. Sometimes it is tearful. Sometimes it is cheerful. But always it is with love. How fortunate my son and grandchildren have been to have had her as a mate and mom. There is joy in gratitude even when there is pain.

Life is like a book ...

LIFE TO ME IS MUCH LIKE A BOOK. IT CAN HOLD MANY PAGES, MANY chapters. Life's book cannot be edited. There is no going back, though through hindsight, there can be changes made as the author moves forward. The pages reveal the joy, the laughter, the drama, the tears, the problems, the solutions, the love, the annoyances, and all other happenings that make the story unique. It comes to a climax and brings about an ending. Sometimes moving forward is in the form of a new book that needs to be written because of an unexpected ending to a current story. In my case, my first marriage had taken me into a wonderful cast of characters who accepted me into their family, but the plot was not managed properly. A divorce followed and dropped me instantly out of that setting. However, I will always treasure the time spent with them, especially my father-in-law Charlie. He was a gentleman through and through. I loved him. He was a wonderful role model for my boys. After his wife Edna passed, we had ample time to chat. He told me he had read the Bible cover-to-cover three times while sitting with his wife each night while she brushed her hair. I felt his love for her and the sadness of his loss. Like my father, he wasn't too sure if there is an afterlife, but we talked about the possibilities. I was with him the evening before he passed. He was hospitalized and semi-conscious with labored breathing. I sat beside him and took his hand in mine. At my touch, he opened his eyes wide and smiled at me. He clearly said, "You were right. I am going to see Edna." He closed his eyes and his labored breathing resumed. I sat with him for a while. When I left, I told him I would see him the next day and kissed him on the forehead. There was no response. I knew he had already said good-bye with clarity. I received the call in the morning that he had joined Edna in spirit. And in the sadness, I felt his joy.

My brother-in-law was the best. Anyone reminiscing time spent with him would be wearing a smile. I can still laugh at his shenanigans. He could be quite a prankster, so I was more than surprised when he appeared to me in spirit and told me to keep writing. He is probably the least likely person I would have expected to hear from. The memory brings me joy.

Divorce does not need to be ugly. It is between two people who are trying to repair the direction of their lives. It is expected that family will support family and perhaps take sides. There was a short time when I was 'out', as they say, but when the shock of the separation and the dust subsided, my place in the family had survived. Our paths have taken different routes through the years, but the link to family is sound. It may seem odd to some, but the ending of my marriage yielded a strong, positive friendship for my husband and me that could not exist in our marriage. Along with the blessing of my two sons, that was my positive outcome to a negative situation.

At the time of my separation, I began journaling my feelings. It was an act of expression very different from my penchant for writing stories that taught or entertained children. There was no Earthly ear to bend. We both were very private about our personal life and went months before family members figured out that we had separated. I was basically alone to iron out my problems. So, I let all my anger, frustration, disappointment, and pain spill out of my pen onto the pages of my journal. I also logged what I felt were strengths and weaknesses for both of us and tried to see where we mismanaged our plot. My simple conclusion to a complex situation was that we were two good people that made better friends than partners. About two years later, I burned the journal. It no longer served me. Life is about choices, and I chose to be happy. My journaling continues to this day with an emphasis on positive entries and outcomes. Perhaps someday my sons will smile while discovering the many unexpected aspects of who I am and what makes me happy. My uniqueness brings me joy.

It took a few years before I started my new book. It had been just plain unthinkable to move into another relationship after my separation from my husband. I was quite happy being me with no interference. There was much pressure of "I know someone…" from acquaintances who meant well. My closer friends knew I would move forward when ready. The time did come when I decided I would accept a date. It was a fix-up and turned out to be a definite set back. To be fair, I'm very sure I was not his cup of tea either. We managed to be polite and had a few interesting exchanges of conversation. The decision to try again is what prompted me to talk to God first and ask to connect with a person who would be kind and respectful and accept who I am, as I am. In return, I vowed to be kind and respectful, and accept him as he is. Request granted. By marrying Carl, I have not only gained two daughters and four more grandchildren, but I also have enjoyed a peaceful thirty-five years (so far) with a kind, caring man. He isn't particularly aware that he has been writing his new book along with me, but he is. The plot in each of our books has the same main characters and is flowing nicely so far. Even so, our journeys are truly unique to each of us. My Self is restored and doing well, and so it seems to be for him. It brings me joy.

Health ...

I HAVE BEEN CONTINUOUSLY BLESSED WITH GOOD HEALTH. I AM active, but not athletic. Now that I am an octogenarian, walking is perfect exercise for me. On one of my walks, I had an amusing flashback to when I was in my late thirties. In one of my moments of gratitude for my good health, I decided to take up jogging to preserve it. My neighbor gave me a beginner's plan. Up until then my exercise level was a comfortable stroll, but please allow me to add that I could stroll a great distance and enjoyed every step of the way while soaking in my surroundings. Somehow, in a moment of insanity, I agreed to take on instruction that I worried would no doubt lead to the saying "no pain, no gain." It was time to crank up the exercise. I could do it. After all, life is about choices and I made a choice.

The plan was for me to walk from one telephone pole to the next; then jog to the next pole; then walk to the next. The pattern would simply be walk, jog, walk, jog. I was to follow that pattern until I was comfortable with it. I did it for two weeks, four poles, eight run-and-jogs. Next step, new pattern: walk one pole, jog two poles, walk one pole, jog two poles. That was a big next step for me. I was somewhat mortified doing the first step with traffic driving by and looking at me. I felt awkward and clumsy. Now I had to jog twice the distance. It was difficult, but I did it. When I collapsed on the couch at the end of day one, new plan, I thought maybe I should leave the jogging to people who have a passion for it. Passion was not what I was feeling. I embarrassed myself gasping for air, red-faced, and certainly not moving with the grace of a gazelle out in public. That thought was validated by my ten-year-old son who supported my efforts, but was upset to see me exhausted, lying in a heap on the couch. That was when he announced, "I love you, Mom, and if you pass out on the road, I will call an ambulance, but I won't tell them you're my mother." We both started laughing and laughing and laughing.

There was nothing wrong with discovering that jogging was not meant to be on my path. It was a distraction. I tried it. It was not for me. I was relieved. When I see joggers running along the road, I admire their passion and fortitude, but have no desire to join them. A wave and thumbs up gives them a nod of support. I applaud the efforts of marathon runners who are striving for their personal best. Each of us is led to achieving our personal best in a way that is right for us. Divine Design will reveal it. Be patient.

Sedona Vortex ...

TRAVEL IS A WONDERFUL MEANS OF EXPANDING YOUR BELIEF SYSTEM. My husband and I traveled to Arizona with our friends Tony and Evelyn. Evelyn and I are like-minded friends. Our spiritual journey has been quite similar over the years of our long friendship. We can look back and ahead as suggested by our astrological sign Gemini. Our husbands also have interests in common. Both were in the Air Force, both have a financial background, and both are open-minded, good sports that indulge their wives. We travel well together, and when we do, laughter prevails. Finding good traveling companions is truly a gift for which the four of us are grateful. We share good memories.

We were on a bus tour. Evelyn and I had a primary goal for this leg of the trip. We planned to visit a vortex while in Sedona. A vortex is often described to be a swirling center of energy that is conducive to healing, meditation, and self-exploration. Its energy mixes with your personal energy field, which is your aura. Our husbands were game, but not necessarily believers. They did not need to believe. If they were ready to experience an energy change, they would. If not, that would also be correct in the moment.

Upon arrival, we sought out a tour guide who would take us to some of the vortexes for which Sedona is well-known. (The grammatical plural is vortices but is not widely used.) The next morning, our guide picked us up in an open red Jeep Wrangler and told us to hold on because there were no paved roads where we were going. The scenery was so different from our surroundings back in New England. Though it had its own beauty, I love the green New England countryside. We were on dusty dirt trails spotted with stubby pine tree growth, red rock, and red sand. The red rock color comes from the high iron content in the sand.

We were able to experience Cathedral Rock, Bell Rock, and Boynton Canyon, three popular sites. The driver was well-versed on the history of each vortex and allowed us to explore and/or meditate during an allotment of leisure time that was factored into the tour. I could feel the energy. It is indescribable, yet palpable. There is a stream below Cathedral Rock that is said to carry healing powers in its water. The flow originates in the red rock mountains which envelop the cathedral. I had been suffering pain in my right-hand thumb for several days. It was difficult to hold my eating utensils, or even get dressed. The guide told me to swish my hand in the flowing water. The pain ended and has not been a problem since. I know that some will say that it was all in my mind. I also know the rest of my vacation was pain-free. I felt joy.

We had the most time while in Boynton Canyon to find a spot to sit and meditate. (It will be no surprise to tell you our mates went for a walk.) Evelyn found a comfy spot for herself, and I sat a distance away on a flat rock beside a small ponderosa pine tree on the side of a hill. My view was of the mountains on the other side of the vast canyon.

My thoughts were mainly mind-chatter, and I was struggling to receive answers to my numerous questions. I'm a put-it-on-the-back-burner girl who uses the busy-ness of life as an excuse to put things on hold. This seemed like the perfect time to remove the simmering pots. When I commented that I didn't want to hold anger towards the two people who supposedly loved me the most, but also hurt me the most, I got an unexpected response. Instantly, a red streak of fire-energy (?) shot across the canyon and burned itself into my heart. It felt hot and searing, yet there was no pain attached. In that milli-second of time, I received an explanation for everything I considered negative in my lifetime up to that moment. A peaceful, warm feeling passed through my body. My soul allowed me to know I received a healing while sitting on a hillside in Boynton Canyon. I no longer have anger to suppress, or express. My humanness cannot explain what happened, but all is understood and forgiven. What an amazing experience. Do I still get annoyed? Yes, I am, after all, living a human lifetime, but I also have the capacity to put the circumstances in perspective before it reaches the stage of anger.

Meditation ...

MEDITATION HAS BEEN MY MOST DIFFICULT PROCESS. IT REQUIRES stilling mind-chatter and finding a quiet setting that will allow the higher vibrational thoughts of my soul to come forth. There are a multitude of quiet settings from which to choose, the closest being the swing in my own backyard. I also find a walk along Cape Cod Canal conducive to freeing my mind. But sitting on a bench overlooking the bay is even better. While sitting on a bench, there is no need to maintain a side focus to avoid a human collision while walking.

I am positive I am perpetually in the beginner's class of learning to meditate. Here I am, an octogenarian, certainly old enough to have mastered it by now, still working on establishing consistency. Beginner, or not, I know I have embraced Anoop Kumar, MD's definition of meditation: *Meditation is an introspective technique that increases your awareness of who/what you are, and as a result, of what your abilities are.* Kumar gives three stages for common types of meditation. One is observing your thoughts and feelings as they surface. Check. I can differentiate between the mind-chatter Ego throws in and other thoughts that surface. The second stage given is observing silence. He points out that there is a space (silence) between the chatters

95

provided by Ego that opens wider as you continue to practice stilling your mind. Check. I am aware of the silence. His third stage is losing yourself. Check. I am convinced I have surpassed my human lower-vibration and connected with my higher-self on many occasions. Still, there is a feeling of frustration when I set out to meditate. I want the connection to be immediate. That is Ego rearing its head.

It was suggested by Suzanne Giesemann at the retreat in North Carolina that we set aside a specific time and space strictly for meditation. The time frame can start at three to five minutes and increase by another minute, and then another as you succeed quieting your mind and begin to sense a response from spirit. I tried her approach and it worked for me. My downfall has been the lack of consistency and self-discipline to meditate daily. It needs to be the same time, same place daily, if you are serious. Initially what you 'hear' will be questioned by you. It means you are on tract. Experiment to find the place and time frame that is suited best for you. It will bring you joy.

There are dozens of reasons one would want to meditate. To reduce anxiety tops the list. Finding a connection to spirit is another. Whatever your reason, you will discover a lot about your Self, which by dictionary definition, is one's own person as being distinct from others. You are unique. Rejoice in knowing that to be truth.

Depending on the ability of the meditator, meditation can be achieved under any circumstances. I found that anything I focus on stops the chatter. So, when I focus on a puzzle, or crochet a blanket, or paint, those activities become a quiet background to my thoughts. What I call fleeting thoughts pop up and I acknowledge them. Surely someone's name has flashed in your mind, and you became aware that you had not seen or heard from that person for a while. It is intuition knocking on your door. Give the person a call. It will also qualify as a RAK.

Meditation is a respite from the hubbub of daily life. It takes practice, practice, practice. Even a minute or two of stilling the mind brings peace and seems to lower anxiety. That makes the commitment worthwhile.

Word of the year ...

FOR 2022, MY WORD(S) FOR THE YEAR WERE *THANK YOU*. I WAS FOCUSED on making sure I recognized and acknowledged all instances that deserved a thank you. I was astounded at how many times I spoke those two words, and how many times I heard those two words. Then again, Auntie Hekkie spent quite a few years instilling good manners and gratitude in me. I found so much joy in consciously expressing thanks all year long. In fact, it led me to this year's word, *joy*.

Joy is my balancing act for 2023. As demonstrated within these pages, joy can be found in all situations, even a loss. It is usually a playful, light feeling that, like a helium balloon, might slip your grasp and float away while you are trying to brush away something heavier. Make a choice to find the joy and hang on to the string. Be like Johnny Mercer and Ac-*cent-tchu- ate the Positive*. Though it is not always apparent, it is there. Believe and trust.

My intention for writing my story is to bring a non-threatening, light-hearted, positive depiction of how spirit weaves its signs into events that occur in our lives. Look for them and allow them to nourish your journey. I am but one of God's many children, only known in celebrity status to Him. There is no status higher than that position, so I am chancing that others less known to the public also have a voice to be heard that will help someone climb a step or two on the spiritual ladder, a ladder that leads to the Light, and God.

Please understand that I have a great respect for celebrity authors who disclose their spiritual beliefs. It is not an easy decision. Their lives are repeatedly scrutinized by a fickle public. It takes notable courage to risk opening yourself to the criticism of non-believers. I must admit not every morsel of information placed on my plate was swallowed in a gulp. I have deflected some concepts which, surprisingly, took on new meanings later in life and became a part of my own philosophy. They resonated with my soul. I have no trouble distinguishing between what is comfortable for me to embrace, and what is questionable and requires a closer look. It is a lifetime of learning. I take time to process a new concept and then file the results in my spiritual filing cabinet along with Trust, Faith, and Joy.

As stated earlier, my Earth Journey has had some crooked paths, some hills to climb, some holes to climb out of, some disappointments and some sadness, all offset by moments of joy. Divine Guidance always gently pushes me in the direction that is right for me; always brings me comfort in the hard times; and kindly gives me the capacity to forgive and be grateful. When I am through, I will be a Soul whose Earth experience expanded its Spiritual Being, and I will happily go back into the Light.

It is not my intention to convince you that I have connected to spirit. Rather, I hope that some of the experiences and explorations into spirit I have shared will align with, and validate, some of yours.

Although I believe everyone can connect with spirit, I also know that everyone is not inclined to do so. No one is wrong. Our Earth journey progresses within the parameters of Divine Design.

May your journey include a multitude of moments which will allow you to *Breathe In the Joy*. Namaste.

Printed in the United States
by Baker & Taylor Publisher Services